THE SIBERIAN HUSKY

Able Athlete, Able Friend

MICHAEL JENNINGS

HOWELL BOOK HOUSE

NEW YORK

For Bev & Dick ~
All the best

Michael ...

Howell Book House
An Imprint of Macmillan General Reference USA
A Pearson Education Macmillan Company
1633 Broadway
New York, NY 10019-6785

Macmillan Publishing books may be purchased for business or sales promotional use. For information please write: Special Markets Department, Macmillan Publishing USA, 1633 Broadway, New York, NY 10019-6785.

ISBN 1-58245-046-3

MACMILLAN is a registered trademark of Pearson Education.

Library of Congress Catalog Card Number: 99-64199.

Manufactured in the United States of America
10 9 8 7 6 5 4 3 2 1

Cover and book design by George J. McKeon

Contents

Foreword

Anyone who has ever fallen in love with a Siberian Husky will want to read *The Siberian Husky: Able Athlete, Able Friend* by Michael Jennings. Unlike any previous book published on the Siberian, this fascinating book includes something for everyone. Whether you're a new admirer of the breed or a longtime devotee, this book will hold your interest from start to finish.

After nearly thirty years developing his own very superior line of Siberians that consistently win in the show ring and excel on the trail, it is clear that Michael writes from a deep love of his chosen breed. He fully appreciates the dogs' athleticism and beauty as defined by the Official Standard, as well as the charming, subtle, sometimes clownish behavior that is quintessentially Siberian.

Michael's introduction stresses both the "magic" of the breed and its limitations. The chapters that follow, whether written by Michael or other "breed experts," are highly informative regarding every essential subject from housetraining to race training, and a special chapter which documents one man's Iditarod experience will absorb you totally. From choosing a puppy to judging in the conformation ring, everything you want in a breed book is here for you.

As one reaches Appendix C, Mike's wonderful descriptions of the Siberian personality will hold the reader spellbound. Those of us who are owned by them will smile as we relive the antics he describes. How fortunate we are to have this author in love with Siberians, for Michael Jennings has beautifully described for us the devotion we all feel for this most intriguing of dogs.

Indeed, whether you have shared your life with Siberians for many years, are considering a Siberian, have just gotten your first puppy, or simply want to learn more about these great dogs, you will definitely want this book as an ideal reference and ongoing joy.

BY PHYLLIS BRAYTON

(Phyllis Brayton has owned and bred Siberian Huskies since 1946. She has served the Siberian Husky Club of America in many capacities, including the presidency, and is currently chairman of the Judges' Education committee. She is one of the breed's most esteemed breeder-judges.)

(Winter Churchill Photography)

Introduction

Every purebred dog is a story, sometimes a very long story. In fact, purebred dogs were in many cases our ancestors' most ingenious inventions, and in some cases that includes Stone Age ancestors. Certainly that is so with the Siberian Husky, a breed probably some 3,000 years old. But to own one is to become part of that story, a history older than recorded human history. And that, when you view it in a certain light, is sort of magical.

In fact, there is much that is magical about the Siberian Husky, and I hope that is partly represented in this book, particularly in the many candid photographs, for certainly the Siberian is a great pleasure to the eye. But I hope there is also much that is simply practical to the raising and training of these sometimes quite mischievous animals who are often hard to outsmart.

Siberians seem a little more primitive, a little closer to wild animals, than most domestic dogs, and owning one or more of them can be a bit more of a challenge. That is one of the basic points of this book. The other is that, once you've accepted and adjusted to that fact, it can be fun and rewarding in ways you never quite imagined. The breed comes, quite literally, almost from the dawn of man and remains, in some ways, almost as inscrutable. Yet few breeds make people laugh more or are quite as much fun simply to watch as are Siberians. Their grace and athleticism is often awe-inspiring, and their gregarious charm is utterly infectious.

I do have a bias, however, and that is to the athlete underneath these beautiful animals—a bias that is no doubt more evident in the slightly more esoteric chapters on breeding, showing and the Standard. In the beginning, the Siberian was a sled dog, and when all is said and done, he should still be a sled dog. If that athlete is allowed to slip out from under those beautiful coats and markings, his health and vigor will vanish, too.

". . . there is much that is magical about the Siberian Husky. . ." (Gene Merritt)

I've collected here some of the most charming, candid photos of Siberians being Siberians I have ever seen collected in one place, and I've asked a number of longtime friends to contribute their expertise in particular chapters: Lois Leonard on "Obedience and Agility," for instance; Pat Tetrault on "The Siberian in the Media"; Jean Fournier and Sarah Gaunt on health care and the special needs of the older Siberian; Jane Steffen on "Sled Training"; Denis Ferentinos and Mary Ferentino on behavioral and training issues; Delbert Thacker and Donna Beckman on the Siberian Husky Club of America; and Peter Johnson on his Iditarod experiences.

I am also grateful to JoLynn Stresing for her wonderful drawings for the Standard analysis section, and to the many other people who contributed photos, information, and advice, particularly photographers Gene Merritt, Joe Asarisi, Cheryl Scheall, Sue Shane, and JoLynn Stresing for the many wonderful images each contributed. I'd also like to thank Karen Morin and Lois Leonard for their help in compiling the appendices.

A breed as popular as the Siberian Husky obviously has something going for it, but popularity alone cannot keep a breed healthy and thriving. There must be a commitment by its fanciers to maintain that health and vigor, to maintain that balance between beauty and athleticism that gives the breed its spirit and its magic. I hope this book helps every friend of the Siberian Husky to keep that essence strong.

(Cheryl Scheall)

Profile of the Siberian Husky—Is It Right for You?

The Siberian Husky is one of the most ancient and noble of all purebred dogs, but he is not the ideal pet for everyone or every family. His sled dog heritage provides him with an innate desire to run, a very high energy level, and a degree of independence that is sometimes maddening. *He typically does not come when he is called,* he loves to dig holes (a denning instinct and survival skill he has apparently inherited from his wild ancestors), and he sheds his profuse coat once or twice a year by the bushel basketful. He is also an escape artist of Houdini-like abilities and *absolutely requires a very secure fenced-in yard or pen,* preferably both. He also, typically, loves everyone, including any potential burglar, thereby rendering him a "hopeless case" as a reliable guard dog.

On the other hand, the Siberian Husky is remarkably intelligent (some say at times *too* intelligent for his own good), clownish and charming. He loves children and is extremely sweet and gentle with them (though puppies and toddlers are not usually a good mix unless well-supervised, since neither quite understands the fragility of the other). He is extremely clean and odorless, making him an excellent choice as a companion for those with any tendency to dog-related allergies. Not surprisingly, a healthy Siberian can live happily out of doors in temperatures down to −60°, if properly sheltered. And, despite his independence and occasional stubbornness, he is an extremely affectionate animal who, even in adulthood, often believes he was born to be a lap dog.

Those who love the Siberian Husky typically cherish his wolf-like, natural beauty and athleticism, his minimal grooming needs, and his strong pack instincts. In a single-dog household, he can sometimes grow restless, bored, and lonely, and so will need to be with his family much of the time. Though Siberians bark very infrequently (a true bark being a territorial signal more common to herding or guard dogs), they will yip if excited or howl if lonely; so lonely Siberians can become quite noisy.

Siberians have strong "pack-drive." (Jack Steffen)

A WORD ABOUT PACK-DRIVE AND PREY-DRIVE

The commonest mistake dog owners make is to think of their dogs as hairy little people. But dogs, in fact, do not operate quite the way people do. They have no concept of democracy, for instance, and only understand the hierarchy of pack structure. It is, therefore, useful to mention the two great motivating forces in dog behavior, and to explain their relevance to the Siberian Husky specifically. Later chapters will explore these concepts more thoroughly, but for now a brief sketch will do.

Typically, what endears us to dogs is their "pack-drive," those instincts which lead them to be good members of our families: the desire to please us, to fit in, to love and be loved. Siberians, unlike many so-called "one-man dogs," have a very strong pack drive. They have a strong need for family, either human or canine, and if they don't have that, they are not happy. Many families discover, for instance, that after their puppy has grown up a bit, say at about a year, it is useful to acquire a second dog to keep the first company and to take some of the social burden off the human members of the family. A single Siberian needs lots of attention—lots of walks, play, exercise—while a pair of Siberians demands much less simply because they have each other. It is probably not advisable, however, to acquire two at the same time, unless they are older, because, with less human interaction, they are likely to become "wild Indians," a sort of law unto themselves.

Equally important, in terms of pack-drive, is a high degree of consistency of training and

*Siberians require the space and opportunity to run.
(Carol Marcy)*

reinforcement by every member of the family. Biting and "mouthing," for instance, is a common mode of play among puppies in a litter, and it is important that every member of the family reinforce a "no biting" rule as it pertains to humans. All it takes is one member of the family who likes to tussle roughly with a puppy to let that puppy believe that using his mouth is an appropriate mode of human interaction, usually with disastrous results: torn clothes or worse. And the same is true of every other activity where the family and family dog interact; there must be uniform reinforcement of all household rules. Consistency and firmness must be the rule. Allowing the dog to sit on the couch with you one day and reading him the riot act the next time he tries it is just a bad idea. Inconsistency leads to a confused and unhappy dog—and an unhappy human pack.

"Prey-drive," on the other hand, is what we, as owners, often find the most frustrating side of normal canine behavior. It is what leads the Siberian with years of Obedience training to still bolt after the squirrel across the road. It is what leads the free-roaming Siberian to raid garbage cans, kill chickens, goats, sheep, and whatever else he can run down—often leading to the local police having to come and shoot the dog. Prey-drive in the Siberian Husky is among the strongest of all breeds simply because for centuries in their native land these dogs were released during the summer months to hunt as packs over the tundra, and those instincts remain strong to this day. Inevitably, some new owners believe all dogs are behaviorally the same, and that they can train any dog to stay close to home. When it comes to Siberians, they are simply wrong, and, as a result, hundreds of Siberians are killed each year because of the arrogance of these uninformed owners.

But when you interact with your Siberian in any number of activities, you may engage and make use of both these inherent drives. Driving a dog team, for instance, is a lot like going hunting with wolves. The dogs thrill to the chase, and you, as pack leader, may also thrill to this primordial urge. And even in less obviously predatory activities—backpacking, skijoring, Obedience or Agility training, or showing in the conformation ring—food used as reinforcement does wonders for the dog's desire to perform. Working dogs are happiest when working, and Siberians, despite their clownish tendencies and sometimes apparently anarchical spirits, are happiest when asked by their masters to do a task for which they have been lovingly and patiently trained.

Siberians are never happier than when working. (Joe Asarisi)

OWNING A SIBERIAN IS NOT EASY

Because of his need for a fenced-in yard, his activity and social needs, the Siberian is not for those who want a cuddly Christmas puppy that they can pretty much leave to his own devices after a few weeks of focused attention. In many ways, a Siberian remains a puppy until he's about 7 years old. A Siberian is a definite *presence* in a household. He will not disappear into the woodwork. His capacity for mischief, when unsupervised, is legendary. But for those who have both a sense of humor and a sense of discipline, who enjoy a bit of a challenge, who love the beauty and tradition of this tough, versatile, very medium-sized animal with perhaps the noblest history of human service of any breed, the Siberian offers sturdy health, long life, and loads of fun, even if that fun is sometimes at his owner's expense.

(Winter Churchill Photography)

CHAPTER 2

History of the Siberian Husky

IN SIBERIA

The history of the Siberian Husky is one of the most fascinating and compelling of any purebred dog. Developed over a period of perhaps 3,000 years by the Chukchi and related peoples of northeastern Siberia, the breed evolved to fill a distinct niche in Chukchi life and culture. In a climate described by many as the most inhospitable in the world, with winter temperatures plummeting to −100°F with wind squalls up to 100 mph, the dogs became the very essence of survival, a tool of remarkable ingenuity. They could travel in large teams of as many as twenty or more out over the ice to allow a single man to ice-fish and return with his catch, sometimes covering as much as 100 miles in a single day. They were small by sled dog standards because the size of the teams minimized per-dog pulling power, while smaller frames maximized endurance and low energy consumption. (Even today, in long races, Siberians consume only about one-half the food their cousins the Alaskan Huskies require.)

Integral as they were to the survival of the tribe, the dogs became central to both the economy and religious life of the Chukchi. The richest members of the community had the best dogs, and they were rich precisely because of this. Religious ceremonies and iconography revolved around the dogs, two of which were purported to guard the gates of heaven, turning away any who had shown cruelty to a dog during their lives. Chukchi legend even held that during a period of famine that decimated both human and dog populations, the last two remaining pups were nursed at a woman's breast to insure the survival of the breed.

Indeed, it was probably the participation of all members of the tribe in this "dog culture" that helped the Siberian Husky become such a remarkable breed. The women reared the pups and chose the "keepers," discarding all but the most promising bitches and neutering all but the most promising males. The men then did the sled training, using mostly the geldings, but many of the dogs continued to sleep indoors with their

families and act as companions for the children. Night temperatures were even measured in terms of the number of dogs necessary to keep a body warm: hence the derivation of the term "three-dog night" (or colder). This process, of course, led to the development of animals of legendary sweetness of temperament, and this was no accident. Because a single man with twenty dogs, 100 miles out on the ice, simply does not get home if there's a dog fight (again, one of the reasons for using geldings; the other being lowered food consumption).

During the winter months, all dogs but the unneutered males were tied up when not working, but these elite dogs were allowed to wander and breed at will, thus insuring that only the very best perpetuated the breed. During the summer, all dogs were cut loose and allowed to hunt in packs, only returning to the villages when the snow returned and prey grew scarce. This no doubt explains the still-intact primitive hunting instincts found in the breed today. (A number of years ago a family's pet Siberian bitch was lost during an autumn

Leonhard Seppala and his Siberians, winners of the All Alaska Sweepstakes in 1915 and 1916, pictured at the "Ruby Derby" in 1916. Note the dogs' height on leg.

John Johnson, the "Iron Man," with two of his lead dogs. Kolma, the most notable, is at left.

hike in the Rockies, only to walk back out of the woods the next spring, a little thin but none the worse for wear, when her family returned in the unlikely hope of finding her. She had not only managed to feed herself, but had also avoided being eaten by coyotes, mountain lions, and other predators.)

In the nineteenth century, the Chukchi faced a peril even deadlier than the Siberian winters in the form of Czarist troops sent on a mission to open the area to the fur trade, and on the all-out genocide of the Chukchi people in the process.

But again, the dogs saved them. Able to outrun the Russian reindeer cavalry on their sleds, the Chukchi managed to evade the invading armies until finally, in a battle not unlike the Battle of the Little Big Horn, the Chukchi, armed only with spears, managed to trap and rout a much larger, heavily armed force of Russian troops, thereby gaining, through a treaty, independence within Czarist Russia—the only tribe ever to do so.

Sadly, in the twentieth century, the Soviets managed to open free trade with the Chukchi, by then known as the "Apaches of the North," eventually introducing smallpox that decimated the tribe. With a diabolical understanding of the place of the dogs in Chukchi cultural coherence, the Soviets then executed the village leaders, who were of course the dog breeders, and set up their own dog breeding programs designed to obliterate the native gene pool and replace it with one that would produce a much larger freighting dog thought to be more effective for their own proposed fur-trading practices in the region. They even went so far, in 1952, as issuing an official proclamation that the breed we now call the Siberian Husky never really existed.

Today, we do know some remnant of the breed still survives in its native territory. The painter Jon Van Zyle has managed to bring back several from the region, and anyone ever witnessing the old *National Geographic Special* on the Siberian tiger will have noticed that one of the two dogs used in the tracking and pursuit of one of these animals was undoubtedly a Siberian Husky.

IN ALASKA

Fortunately, the reputation of the little Chukchi dogs had already spread throughout the world long before the Soviets managed to relegate them to the category of "those who officially never existed." By the turn of the twentieth century, polar exploration had captured public imagination worldwide, and adventurers came to the yearly Markova Fair on the Siberian peninsula where tribes of the area came to trade. This gathering included the Chukchi and other dog-breeding tribes, such as the Koryak (all of whom probably had some part in the pool of animals that eventually became the Siberian Husky). In 1908, a Russian fur trader named Goosak acquired a team there and, in 1909, took them across the Bering Strait to race in the newly established All Alaska Sweepstakes, a 408-mile, grueling race first run in 1908. The Alaskan Gold Rush had established the sled dog as an invaluable commodity, and the race had been instituted to add excitement to an otherwise pretty grim world, to give bragging rights to the eventual winner, and to give vent to that favorite frontier boomtown passion, gambling.

The race went from Nome to Candle and back, crossing every conceivable terrain, including a valley almost always engulfed in a blizzard. Caches of food were strategically hidden along the way by the individual drivers. Regular checkpoints were established, but the duration of rest were at each driver's discretion. Bets were placed at the Board of Trade Saloon in Nome, and betting was open until the first team crossed the finish line. Schools were let out for the four days of the race,

and at the start of the 1909 event, there was already more than $100,000 on the books.

About half the weight of the local sled dogs, and much smaller in stature, the Siberian entry, referred to then as Siberian Wolf Dogs, was given little chance by oddsmakers. "Siberian Rats," they were dubbed because of their diminutive size. But Goosak was able to convince a driver named Thurstrup to take on the team. So, on a cold, bleak morning in April 1909, the first team of Siberian Huskies to be seen on the North American continent loped out of the town of Nome and into the annals of history.

As it turned out, Thurstrup was not a wise or judicious driver. Seeing himself with the opportunity to take the lead at the halfway point in the race, he cut short his rest period in Candle, only to be overtaken by two more rested teams in the last stretch of the race. But a third place finish by the little dogs astonished everyone and inspired a young Scot named Fox Maule Ramsey to acquire some seventy new Siberians from across the Bering Sea, spending $25,000 on a freighter to transport them. Dividing these into three teams for the 1910 race, he managed to capture first, second, and fourth place finishes.

The team finishing first in this 1910 race was driven by the legendary John "Iron Man" Johnson, who completed the race in 74 hours, 14 minutes, 37 seconds. This time was never equaled, even when the race was rerun within the last decade with the benefit of modern equipment, better nutrition, and supposedly more specialized hybrid "race dogs."

Over the next few years, scandal plagued the race, with rumors that Johnson's dogs had been drugged near the end of the race or that the moneyed interests had actually convinced him to throw the race, and it was not until 1914 that Johnson again won the event.

Enter a Little Man with His Little Dogs

Leonhard Seppala was born in Skjervoy, Norway, inside the Arctic Circle, and came to Alaska as a young man around 1900 seeking fortune and adventure. Though only about 5 feet tall, he had been an Arctic fisherman since the age of 11, an apprentice blacksmith to his father, and was an accomplished wrestler and skier. He worked at various jobs in the mining camps until, in 1914, his employer, Jafet Lindeberg, acquired what was left of the first Siberian imports and their offspring, about fifteen animals in all, as a proposed gift to the explorer Captain Roald Amundsen, who was planning a dash to the North Pole. Seppala was entrusted with the care and training of the dogs, and he took to it with relish.

As luck would have it, the outbreak of World War I changed Amundsen's plans, and Seppala ended up in possession of the dogs. He entered the 1914 All Alaska Sweepstakes, but with disastrous results: He lost the trail, his dogs' feet got badly cut, and he had to drop out early. But the next year he trained hard and in secret, far from town, winning the 1915 Sweepstakes by over and hour and going away. He repeated this easy victory in 1916 and 1917, at which time the increased war effort and the lack of any real competition for him caused the race to be discontinued.

He remained devoted to his Siberians, however, and over the next few years "the little man with his little dogs," as he came to be called, became a kind of legend in Alaska, hauling freight

During his first trip east, the redoubtable Leonhard Seppala and his celebrated "Serum Run" team posed for this photo on the roof of a department store in Providence, Rhode Island. One of these dogs actually leaped over the roof's guard wall of this very tall building that day. Fortunately, he was saved when his fall was broken by a projecting awning.

Togo, leader in the serum drive.

A contrast of styles—Leonhard Seppala (left) and Arthur Walden (right) and their leader dogs pose with their racing trophies in this intriguing vintage study.

and supplies, setting many new records in mid-distance races, and on several occasions being involved in truly heroic exploits: once, unarmed, chasing down an armed kidnapper, and on another occasion transporting a man mangled in a sawmill accident over a long distance at a speed no one thought possible.

It wasn't until 1925, however, that Seppala and his Siberians came to national prominence, with the famous "Serum Run" that saved the city of Nome from a diphtheria epidemic. Seppala and his Siberians, with his famous lead dog Togo, covered

340 miles in that race against death, with no other team traveling more than 53 miles. Togo, a dog which Seppala credited with over 5,000 miles in his running career, became permanently lame from that marathon run, so it is sadly ironic that one of

Seppala's scrub dogs, Balto, who only traveled the last 50 miles, should have gotten most of the credit. The newspaper writers simply liked his name more, so it was his statue erected in New York City's Central Park, made from children's donated pennies, and he who became the star in the recent Disney movie. The teams had covered a distance of 650 miles that normally took the mail teams twenty-five days, and they did it in just five and a half days. Senator Dill of Washington state had the story written into the *Congressional Record,* one sentence of which reads, "Men had thought the limit of speed and endurance had been reached in the grueling races of Alaska, but a race for sport and money proved to have far less stimulus than this contest; in which humanity was the urge and life was the prize."

Later, when the statue of Balto was erected in Central Park, a plaque was attached, which read:

Dedicated to the indomitable spirit of the sled dogs that relayed antitoxin six hundred miles over rough ice across treacherous waters through arctic blizzards to the relief of stricken Nome in the winter of 1925.

Endurance

Fidelity

Intelligence.

IN NEW ENGLAND

The Scrum Run made Seppala a national hero and brought him to the lower 48 to march in parades and pose for glamorous photographs in his equally

Elizabeth Ricker (later Nansen) with a group of famous early sled dogs. In the foreground, from left, are Sugruk, Mukluk and Sapsuk II. The dogs in the background are Jean (left) and Sepp I. (Warren Boyer)

glamorous furs, sometimes in 90°F weather. It also brought a challenge from the polar explorer, adventurer, and full-time blowhard, Arthur Walden, to come to New England to race against his locally famous Chinook dogs, a strain of large, Mastiff-types he had developed from a single dog. This dog, named Chinook, gained fame on Admiral Richard E. Byrd's first Antarctic expedition. Walden would become Byrd's chief dog handler on that voyage, was the president of the New England Sled Dog Club, and was generally considered unbeatable.

The last of the imports, circa 1930. Kreevanka is the light dog at far left, Tserko is the dark dog at far right.

chief dog handler and a two-time Congressional Medal of Honor winner (once for saving the Admiral's life and once for his search-and-rescue missions during the Battle of the Bulge), was a teenager at the time. Moulton remembered vividly the stark contrast between the dogs as the two teams were boarded at opposite ends of a barn the night before the race. "At one end," he says, "were Walden's great big Chinooks, while at the other were these sweet, little, kind of foxy Siberian dogs who stood up on their hind legs to greet you, and their heads were hardly higher than your waist."

What was not quite understood in 1925, however, was that as you double a dog's size, you only increase heart and lung capacity by about a third; so big dogs tire much sooner than medium-sized dogs. Seppala simply "blew the doors off" Walden's team the next day, changing the history of New England sled dog racing for all time.

Admiral Byrd, himself, would learn the same lesson when he reprimanded Moulton, upon first arriving on his second Antarctic expedition, asking why in the world he had brought such little dogs. Moulton simply demurred, and Byrd then took off

Seppala accepted the challenge, but was sly as they drove their teams for three days to get to the site of the race, keeping his dogs in check and letting Walden gain a false sense of confidence. After all, Seppala knew his dogs to be out of condition from all their parade appearances and wasn't sure how they would perform on the New England trails. The contrast between the two teams was striking: the Chinooks weighing in at 90 to 100 pounds, the Siberians at around half that weight. In fact, many New Englanders objected to the race on humanitarian grounds, considering the Siberians too small to compete. Dick Moulton, who would later become Byrd's for several days on an exploratory foray, leaving the dogs and men to unload the ship. Upon his return, he again sent for Moulton, this time apologizing profusely, explaining that the men had told him that the little dogs had displayed a strength and endurance that seemed nothing short of miraculous.

Moulton gives a little grin at this point in the story, a twinkle in his eyes. "You see," he says, "I knew that not only do big dogs get tired quickly, they also need a long time to rest. But I wasn't going tell HIM that!"

This historically significant photo, circa 1932, includes the important early Siberians (from left) Bonzo, Toto, Suggen, Sepp II, Kingeak, Snegruf, Tserko, Kreevanka, and Smokey of Seppala. The driver is Harry Wheeler and his passenger is Charlie Belford, both famous drivers. The type and body proportion appears lovely on these animals, but especially so on Suggen, Tserko, and Kreevanka.

Early New England Breeders

The Last of the Imports, and AKC Recognition

Seppala stayed on in New England for a time, winning pretty much all the races and planting the seeds of the future Siberian Husky that would come to be officially recognized by the American Kennel Club in 1930. He formed a partnership with a woman named Elizabeth Ricker, an avid sled dog enthusiast, who imported the last Siberians to come directly from Siberia. Nine of these were selected by the renowned expert on Siberian dogs,

Olaf Swenson, but the ship that brought them to the United States became stranded in ice for the winter, and only four survived. The most influential of these being the males, Kreevanka and Tserko, who, along with the legendary Togo, his father Suggen, and the beautiful leader Fritz, probably figure in the pedigree of every Siberian Husky living—if one were to trace back that far.

The dogs developed by the Seppala-Ricker partnership eventually went to Harry Wheeler of St. Jovite, Canada, in 1932 when Elizabeth Ricker married the explorer Kaare Nansen and gave up her dogs. From these, in turn, came the animals that would form the three most influential kennels in the establishment and development of the

Milton Seeley with Toska of Wonalancet (right) and her sister Cherie. Toska was the dam of Ch. Wonalancet's Baldy of Alyeska.

AKC-recognized Siberian Husky: Milton and Eva Seeley's Chinook Kennels, Nicholas and Lorna Demidoff's Monadnock Kennels, and Mrs. Marie Lee Frothingham's Cold River Kennels.

Chinook

Milton and Eva Seeley acquired Chinook Kennels from Arthur Walden shortly after his return from the Antarctic on the first Byrd expedition. This was in 1929. Milton had just been diagnosed with diabetes and was advised by his doctor to take up country living. It was at Chinook that the dogs were trained for Byrd's second and third Antarctic expeditions, and there that most of the Search and Rescue teams used in World War II were developed. Like Elizabeth Ricker before them, the Seeleys bred both Alaskan Malamutes and Siberian Huskies, and are seen as doing much of the important foundation work in both breeds. For their Siberian stock, they combined animals from Harry Wheeler and those coming directly from Alaska to produce several of the first champions in the breed after AKC recognition. Their most famous and influential animals were probably Ch. Wonalancet's Baldy of Alyeska (sire of the extremely influential Izok of Gap Mountain) and Ch. Alyeska's Suggen of Chinook, both of whom proved important to the development of the Demidoffs' Monadnock line along with many others.

Milton Seeley died in 1944, but Eva (affectionately known to all as "Short") continued to be very influential in the breed (judging, driving, breeding, and serving in many capacities for the Siberian Husky Club of America, of which both Seeleys had been founding members) for decades thereafter. When Short Seeley died in 1985, Chinook Kennels became an official historic landmark of the State of Vermont, and can be visited to this day.

Monadnock

If Short Seeley came to be seen as the grandmother of the Siberian Husky, surely Lorna

The legendary Eva "Short" Seeley with Ch. Wonalancet's Baldy of Alyeska and Ch. Wonalancet's Disko of Alyeska.

*Sometimes even Siberians get cold, like these that were with
Admiral Byrd in the Antarctic.*

*This litter, shown in this 1935 photo, marked the beginning of the preeminence
that Monadnock Kennels enjoyed for so many years. The dogs are (from left)
Anvik of Alyeska, Ch. Togo of Alyeska, Waska, Toto, Tosco of Alyeska (the
Monadnock foundation matron), and lying down, Cheeak of Alyeska.*

Lorna Taylor with Ch. Togo of Alyeska, first Siberian Husky to place in the Working Group (Newport, Rhode Island, 1939).

One of the most exquisite of the Monadnock bitches, Ch. Belka of Monadnock II, 1950 SHCA National Specialty winner.

Demidoff was its mother. She became interested in sled dogs while married to Moseley Taylor, owner of the *Boston Globe,* who purchased her first Siberians for her from the Seeleys, along with a dog named Tuck who came from the Mike Cooney/John "Iron Man" Johnson kennels in Alaska. She became the first woman to win a race, finished her first champion (and first Group placer in the breed) in 1939, her first home-bred champion in 1941, and became, for the next three decades, the most prominent breeder of Siberian show dogs and breeding stock in the United States. Having divorced Mosely Taylor, she married Nicholas Demidoff, an émigré Russian prince, in 1941, becoming affectionately known as "the Princess." She fielded competitive teams through the 1950s and continued to drive her pleasure teams until well into her sixties. Her animals probably won more National Specialties than anyone else's before or since, and her Ch. Monadnock's Pando was arguably the most influential stud dog

Probably the most famous photograph in the history of the breed: Monadnock stalwarts, Ch. Monadnock's King, Ch. Monadnock's Pando, and Mulpus Brook's The Roadmaster.

The brace that fired public imagination by capturing Best Brace in Show awards at every major eastern show where they competed, Ch. Monadnock's Pando and Ch. Monadnock's King.

in the history of the breed. (When he was shown for the last time in the Veterans' Class at age 14 in Philadelphia, he not only received a standing ovation, but was discovered to be the progenitor of 100 of the 103 Siberians shown that day!)

With his son, Ch. Monadnock's King, he won every major Best Brace in Show award for which they competed, and virtually spearheaded the black-and-white, blue-eyed fashion in the breed. Lorna once told me the author said she regretted having started "that craze" and also regretted letting Pando be used at stud on so many bitches. "But,

you know," she said, "there were so many shy dogs in those days that if the bitch had a good temperament I usually accepted her for breeding." I think this is a very telling comment because, although she was known (quite rightly) for establishing consistency of type in the breed, her greatest gift was probably in the area of making more consistent the confident, friendly temperament we so much value in the Siberian today. Until her death in 1993, Lorna Demidoff remained the "premier" breeder-judge of Siberians and one of America's most respected Group and Best in Show judges.

Cold River

Mrs. Marie Lee Frothingham, known to her friends as "the Duchess," did not follow her friends Short Seeley and Lorna Demidoff into the show ring, with the consequent stronger focus on greater consistency of type, markings, and furnishings. She did produce several influential show champions, most significantly Ch. Helen of Cold River (Dr. Roland Lombard's great racing leader), but her focus remained racing. Though she never drove a team herself, she fielded some of the most competitive teams of her time, 1936–56, often two top-flight teams per race. When she retired, some of her better animals were passed onto her then driver/trainer team, Lyle and Marguerite Grant, to form their famous Marlytuk Kennels. Many of these dogs, though still very capable running dogs, became dominant show dogs, particularly the multiple-Specialty winner and famous producer, Ch. Marlytuk's Red Son of Kiska, sired by the last great Monadnock stud, Ch. Monadnock's Akela.

Millie Turner Remick with the Cold River Kennels team consisting of (from left) Juneau, Tongass, Ch. Vanka of Seppala II, Putsa of Seppala and Surgut.

OTHER GREAT SIBERIANS AND THEIR PEOPLE

Most of the other talented Siberian fanciers from the decades of the '30s, '40s, and early '50s remained, like Mrs. Frothingham, primarily dedicated to the racing Siberian, the Siberian athlete. Dr. Alec Belford and his son Dr. Charles Belford, both veterinarians, fielded highly competitive teams: Charlie winning something like fifty-seven of the sixty-four races he entered. Roland and Lillian Bowles had much success with their Cal-ivali dogs, as did Bill Shearer with his Foxstand animals. Bill Belletete and J. August ("Tat") Duval, both having been trained with Search and Rescue teams during the war, returned to New England as avid dog drivers. Belletete produced the famous Izok of Gap Mountain, while Duval owned a team of matched, Monadnock Siberians containing the very important Ch. Aleka's Czarina. This team was later owned by Jean Lane, now Jean Bryar—six-time winner of the Womens' North American Championship. It was she who bred Izok to Czarina to produced that famous mainstay in the Monadnock breeding program: Mulpus Brook's the Roadmaster, named after the latest top-of-the-line Buick of the day.

During this period, Earl and Natalie Norris also established their Anadyr line in Alaska in 1946, with foundation stock acquired from Chinook Kennels. Earl helped establish the famous Fur Rendezvous World Championship race and won the event with purebred teams in 1947 and '48, while Natalie won the Women's event in 1954 and the Women's North American Championship in 1970. They also produced the great racing leader, Ch. Bonzo of Anadyr, the first Siberian to win a Best in Show award, as well as the very influential Alaskan's Nicolai II of Anadyr. They continue to field Iditarod teams to this day, as well as providing top racing stock to breeders all over the world.

Dr. Roland Lombard, one of the greatest dog drivers of all time.

Igloo Pak's Tok, from Dr. Lombard's successful kennel, was a strong, positive influence on the Siberian.

Natalie remains active as a conformation judge, as well as being the premier presenter of judges' education programs presented under the auspices of the Siberian Husky Club of America at National Specialties.

Last, but certainly not least, was the incomparable "Doc" Lombard, probably the greatest Siberian driver since Leonhard Seppala. Putting himself through veterinary school on the proceeds he received by winning the handicap race at Laconia at age 19, Dr. Roland Lombard eventually set up practice in Wayland, Massachusetts, in 1940, where, with wife Louise, he established his famous Igloo Pak (meaning "home of the white man")

Kennels. He came to dominate the racing scene in the Northeast and Canada through the 1940s, '50s, and '60s, and then proceeded to do the same thing in the even more challenging races in Alaska throughout the 1970s. More importantly, like Seppala before him, Lombard strove to improve the lot of sled dogs throughout the world, introducing innovations in nutrition, equipment, and care. He continued to race right up until 1987, just three years before his death at age 89. Among his most influential dogs were Igloo Pak's Chukchi, Igloo Pak's Tok, and Igloo Pak's Wing-A, all of which figure prominently among today's racing lines.

So successful were all these enthusiasts of the racing Siberian that, by 1961, Elizabeth Nansen, Seppala's first partner, could claim in an article that the Siberian racing dog had proved itself superior to all comers: this from a tiny gene pool of only thirteen original animals and only a handful of kennels in which to house and breed them. Today, with a U.S. population of Siberians numbering into the tens of thousands, we could not make that claim, for reasons too numerous and too complex to elaborate. But the debt owed by the breed to these people who worked to maintain the native vigor and health of these remarkable Arctic athletes is immeasurable. Even the most exquisite Best-in-Show winning Siberian or the most pampered house pet owes its essential health to the sled dog within it: Lose that health and vigor, and you've lost the Siberian Husky as a breed.

The last of the great Monadnock studs, Ch. Monadnock's Akela.

SOME REFLECTIONS ON THE BREED'S HISTORY

Hardiness, speed, and versatility have been the hallmarks of the breed we today call the Siberian Husky. He had to be hardy enough to survive dreadful Siberian winters and hard work on very little food. He had to have the speed and endurance to travel great distances quickly in his native land and to win races so impressively in Alaska. But he also proved remarkably versatile: many of the same dogs that won 25-mile races in New England also broke 1,400 miles of trail in the Antarctic, often with substantial loads. Today, the Siberian lives in every climate and almost every country in the world, where he is valued as a pet, Obedience dog, Agility competitor, skijoring dog, backpacker, sprint racer, distance racer, Tracking dog, Therapy dog, show dog, and

Combining the best of Monadnock with the best of Marlytuk, Ch. Marlytuk's Red Sun of Kiska was one of the all-time greats, both a show dog and a producer.

probably things I haven't even thought of. And he does all this with a kind of rakish charm that affects those who love and work with him, and maybe it even changes them. Perhaps it's the humor that seems to twinkle out of the depth of Arctic time in his mischievous eyes, or the sheer pleasure he seems to take in work or play or a simple belly rub (or terrorizing the neighbor's cat, for that matter). At any rate, there's something a little magical—even metaphysical—about Siberians, and it seems to rub off on the people who work with them closely.

In speaking of Leonhard Seppala, one New England dog driver described him this way:

That man is superhuman. He passed me every day of the race, and I wasn't loafing any. I couldn't see that he drove his dogs. He just clucked to them every now and then, and they would lay into their harnesses harder than I've ever seen dogs do before. Something came out of him and went into those dogs with that clucking. You've heard of some men who hold supernatural control over others. Hypnotism, I guess you call it. I suppose it's just as likely to work on dogs. Seppala certainly has it if anyone has.

Certainly "Doc" Lombard had the same kind of rapport with his dogs, a deep primitive connection, a pack leader's easy assurance, and almost telepathic ability to communicate, a certain Paleolithic linkage. After he died in 1990, I remembered a time I had spent with him and several other legendary drivers. He had recently suffered a stroke and could no longer speak, but he was anxious for me to understand the issues of form and function they were discussing, and his lack of speech in no way inhibited the obvious rapport he had with his dogs. Three years later I came up with this poem about the event, a tribute to Doc and the magical dogs he helped make famous.

PILGRIMAGE

—*In memory of Roland Lombard, DVM*

I have entered the circle
of old men. They are "talking dogs,"
and I have been invited. Outside
in the October chill, the dogs are restless.
We hear their chains jingling, sense their feet
quick-dancing, their new fur rippling and attentive.
We feel their Asiatic eyes glittering like stars
after first snow, they who come from a world
with 200 words for snow.

          Inside, the first man
speaks. He has a womanizer's easy smile,
a slaver's hard laugh. He's run with the best
and beaten them. He tells of being chased
by wolves, a panicky jab of a ski pole
into the haunch of a dog suddenly crouched
and frightened—the yelp, the burst of speed.
He tells of later fastening that ski pole
to the sled frame just at dog eye-level,
banishing forever the big gray's
shrewd laziness.

          The next draws slow on a cigarette,
speaks slow, tells of 1,400 miles of Antarctic wastes,
crevasses opening like grim mouths, nails
digging in for dear life; the sheer guts, tirelessness,
even the autocratic Byrd's grudging admiration
despite their small frames. He smiles then
and waits for the third

          who cannot speak
but has eyes like blue fire, wolf's eyes

under shaggy white brows—patient, fierce,
yet mild in their singleness of purpose.
That he can no longer speak seems proof
he's gone hunting with wolves, entering
their silence like a furred, ghostly god.
He is legend even among the Inuit
for kindness, for indefatigable attention
to detail—able to enter a dog's mind
and bring out the best in him
with no more than cluck or gesture—
who's felt the wind of the bull moose
charging, the white bear's shadow,
yet come back again and again to beat the best
of the younger men. It is this quiet
the dogs outside are restless for, his quick signal
the hunt is on.

          He has fashioned a model
of scapula, humerus and ulna to show me
the shoulder blade's proper rotation. Outside
he buries my hands in the deep ruff of his leader,
his eyes searching mine for the flicker of
   comprehension.
Each dog, whirling on his chain like a separate
   constellation,
keeps eyes riveted on him, waiting for the touch,
the nod, the signal.

          A gasp goes up
as we peer into the treacherous ravine
that starts his training trail, now over half a
   century old.

"He wants to die on the runners," someone
  whispers.
The first stars have come out, their ancient light
perhaps even colder than wolf's eyes. A hint
of snow's in the air, but also a surge,

electric, similar to a February night
I stepped from a Lakota sweat lodge
and stared into buffalo fire—the horned skull
speaking to the stars.

Discipline, dedication, and the desire to win—Dr. Roland Lombard in action with Ch. Helen of Cold River on lead.

CHAPTER 3

The Official Standard of the Siberian Husky— With Interpretation

A Breed Standard is the written document that guides judges in their selections in the show ring, an attempt to describe the ideal specimen of that breed in terms of type, soundness, and temperament. "Type" refers to those general characteristics of coat, shape of skull, body proportions, and all the other components that make an individual specimen recognizable as a member of its breed. "Soundness" refers to the structural components that enable a dog to function effectively in its defined work and move well in the ring. Good "temperament" begins with the dog not trying to bite the judge in the ring, and varies somewhat thereafter according to the function of the breed.

As stated elsewhere, we are extremely lucky that our earliest Breed Standards were written by people who worked their dogs, and who had seen the animals that came to be called Siberian Huskies since their first arrival on the North American continent. They embraced the great variety of coat color, eye color, and markings they found on these early dogs, and gave their descriptive concentration to issues of type, balance, proportions, and agility they found on these extremely versatile athletes.

Since the first real written Standard of the breed, composed in 1932, the official document has undergone minor revisions and clarifications in almost every decade. In fact, as of this writing, a "Proposed Standard Revision" is under review by the Board of Directors of the Siberian Husky Club of America. In each case, however, the aim of revisions has simply been to more accurately translate into words the specifics already exhibited in those early animals, and to accommodate to new knowledge of dog anatomy. Fashions do change in the show ring from time to time, but unless an individual specimen conforms to the details of the Standard, it is simply not a good Siberian, no matter how fashionable, or how many wins it may acquire. The champion of the late 1930s pictured in this chapter, for example, is as excellent an example of type and body proportions today as he was then.

The current Standard which follows was approved in 1971 and reformatted in 1990.

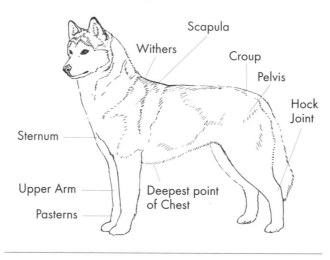

This drawing of a top-winning contemporary Siberian clearly exhibits her near-perfect body proportions. (JoLynn Stresing)

GENERAL APPEARANCE

The Siberian Husky is a medium-sized working dog, quick and light on his feet and free and graceful in action. His moderately compact and well-furred body, erect ears, and brush tail suggest his Northern heritage. His characteristic gait is smooth and seemingly effortless. He performs his original function in harness most capably, carrying a light load at a moderate speed over great distances. His body proportions and form reflect this basic balance of power, speed and endurance. The males of the Siberian Husky breed are masculine but never coarse; the bitches are feminine but without weakness of structure. In proper condition, with muscle firm and well-developed, the Siberian Husky does not carry excess weight.

COMMENT: The Siberian is, quite simply, a dog invented to fill a very specific need, an extremely frugal animal bred for a harsh environment; so underlying this simple description is a prescription for moderation that would please even the staunchest Aristotelian. In the space of several sentences, we find that the Siberian is "medium-sized," "moderately compact," reflects a "balance of power, speed, and endurance," that males are "masculine but not coarse" and bitches "feminine without

Ideal body proportions for a Siberian Husky dog and bitch. (JoLynn Stresing)

weakness of structure," that both should be "dry": carrying no excess weight, not fleshy or loose. We find, also, the reason for this prescription: that the original function of the Siberian was to carry a "light load at moderate speed over great distances." This is a tremendously important phrase in coming to an understanding of the conformation of the Siberian, for although he has gained much recognition for his accomplishments in the area of Arctic and Antarctic exploration, as well as in the field of sled dog racing, he was intended neither as a heavy draft animal nor as a sprinter. He was bred to pull light loads often as much as 100 miles in a single day, a job that required a dog that was "quick and light on his feet and free and graceful in action." Anything clumsy or heavy in movement would be unable to maintain the pace required of these dogs; anything too refined would lack the necessary pulling power and stamina.

SIZE, PROPORTION, SUBSTANCE

Height: Dogs, 21 to 23½ inches at the withers. Bitches, 20 to 22 inches at the withers. *Weight:* Dogs, 45 to 60 pounds. Bitches, 35 to 50 pounds. Weight is in proportion to height. The measurements mentioned above represent the extreme height and weight limits with no preference given to either extreme. Any appearance of excessive bone or weight should be penalized. In profile, the length of the body from the point of the shoulder to the rear point of the croup is slightly longer than the height of the body from the ground to the top of

Ch. Turu of Alyeska, shown outside Sportsman's Show in Boston in 1941 with handler Dr. Roland Lombard, exhibits type and proportion that is as excellent today as it was then. Note, particularly, the angle of croup and pelvis. (From the collection of Louise Lombard, courtesy of Bob Thomas.)

the withers. **Disqualification:** Dogs over 23½ inches and bitches over 22 inches.

COMMENT: Size is as integral a feature of the Siberian as coat texture or ear set, and just as important to his functionality. A dog smaller than that called for by the Standard will lack the necessary strength to be a good sled dog, while a larger individual will lack speed and endurance. So, again, it is the moderate that is required with absolutely no preference given to either extreme set by the

Standard. This is important to realize even though in competition in a large class it is often the larger specimens that stand out immediately simply because of their size. But it is the relative body proportions of dogs within the range of the Standard that should be carefully compared, not the absolute size. It should be remembered that the great leader Togo weighed only 48 pounds, and that current Iditarod dogs tend to weigh in at about 50 pounds. It is also interesting to note that as a possible by-product of this insistence upon the maintenance of medium size, Siberian fanciers have so far avoided many of the problems found in breeds where greater size is preferable. Hip dysplasia and osteochondritis remain relatively rare in this breed.

One of the principal issues under consideration by the Standard Revision Committee is whether the height to length proportions described in this portion of the Standard ought to be made more precise. Studies of hundreds of working Siberians show their lengths (as measured from sternum to pin bone) to be only 7 to 11 percent longer than their height (as measured from withers to ground), with 12 percent being simply too long for endurance. This is an almost square dog, as are most current Iditarod competitors. This same study found leg length to be necessarily at least 10 percent longer than chest depth, as did Curtis Brown's more general studies of endurance gallopers.

HEAD

Expression: Is keen, but friendly; interested and even mischievous. *Eyes:* Almond shaped, moderately spaced and set a trifle obliquely. Eyes may be brown

Outstanding type, proportions, and athletic body on this beautiful, feminine bitch. (Allen Photography)

Pleasing head on a young male, albeit with a slightly blocky muzzle.

or blue in color; one of each or particolored are acceptable.

Faults: Eyes set too obliquely; set too close together.

Ears: Of medium size, triangular in shape, close fitting and set high on the head. They are thick, well furred, slightly arched at the back, and strongly erect, with slightly rounded tips pointing straight up. *Faults:* Ears too large in proportion to the head; too wide set; not strongly erect.

Skull: Of medium size and in proportion to the body; slightly rounded on top and tapering from the widest point to the eyes. *Faults:* Head clumsy or heavy; head too finely chiseled.

Stop: The stop is well-defined and the bridge of the nose is straight from the stop to the tip. *Fault:* Insufficient stop.

Muzzle: Of medium length; that is, the distance from the tip of the nose to the stop is equal to the distance from the stop to the occiput. The muzzle is of medium width, tapering gradually to the nose, with the tip neither pointed nor square. *Faults:* Muzzle

An exquisite male head showing correct eye, stop, and length of muzzle.

Excellent stop and eye set, but a little short in muzzle. (Gene Merritt)

either too snipy or too coarse; muzzle too short or too long.

Nose: Black in gray, tan or black dogs; liver in copper dogs; may be flesh colored in pure white dogs. The pink-streaked "snow nose" is acceptable.

Lips: Are well pigmented and close fitting.

Teeth: Closing in a scissors bite. *Fault:* Any bite other than scissors.

COMMENT: Along with coat type, and general size and proportion of the body, the head is the primary indicator of type in a breed, and thus is an important factor in the assessment of any purebred dog. It has been argued that heads are basically a matter of aesthetic whim and have little to do with the actual functioning capability of a breed. This is, of course, not altogether true.

A Siberian, for instance, would be hard-pressed to survive in an Arctic climate with anything but a well-furred ear, and an argument could probably be made that the smaller ear, as compared to that of the German Shepherd, would be less vulnerable to cold. The erect ear is also more generally efficient than the hanging ear and less prone to infection. It

Lovely head type in a bitch. Note particularly the thick, well-furred ears.

Old-timers in Siberians often say that ear set is more indicative of type than ear height. Though the ears are tall in this dog, head type is otherwise good. (Joe Asarisi)

has further been hypothesized by Richard and Alice Fiennes in their book, *The Natural History of Dogs,* that the well-defined stop called for in the Siberian Husky Standard allows for the maximum development of the frontal sinuses, which trap exhaled warmed air, thereby forming a warm cushion over the delicate tissues of the eyes and forebrain, and also helping warm the cold inhaled air as it passes along the nasal passages. Veteran drivers like Roland Lombard have argued that a muzzle shorter than required by the Standard fails to warm the air sufficiently before entering the sinuses.

The requirement for close-fitting lips addresses a survival need in subzero temperatures, and one feature noted by the earliest fanciers was the dogs' ability to work with their mouths closed, thereby avoiding frostbitten lungs. The scissors bite is the most efficient for tearing food with minimum wear. The medium-sized head, like the medium length of neck called for in a later section of the Standard, is optimal for endurance, the head and neck performing a vital function in the maintenance of balance and the movement of the front assembly. Since it can probably be further argued that the almond-shaped eye called for in the Standard is the one most easily protected between the frontal bones and zygomatic arch (cheekbone), and found most frequently among wild canids, this

Though very pleasing to look at, this bitch has somewhat small, close-set eyes that are not obliquely set, and her ear set appears a bit wide. (Cheryl Scheall)

Tall ears, a bit broad at base, but a lovely, feminine head. (Silja Mikkelsen)

leaves only the slightly oblique eye set and very high ear set called for by the Standard in the realm of simple aesthetic preference. But since these characteristics were found on the majority of early specimens, and since they are among the characteristics distinguishing the Siberian from his cousins, the Alaskan Malamute, Samoyed, and the no longer recognized Eskimo, requiring their maintenance seems eminently justifiable.

Another issue raised by the Standard Review Committee is whether a more blanket endorsement of various eye colors wouldn't be more helpful, such as "eye color immaterial," thus more clearly endorsing the various amber and gold shades consistent with red dogs, and the sometimes even greenish shades created by certain particolored mixtures in the eye.

NECK, TOPLINE, BODY

Neck: Medium in length, arched and carried proudly erect when dog is standing. When moving at a trot, the neck is extended so that the head is carried slightly forward. *Faults:* Neck too short and thick; neck too long.

Chest: Deep and strong, but not too broad, with the deepest point being just behind and level with the elbows. The ribs are well-sprung from the spine but flattened on the sides to allow for freedom of

Another lovely, feminine head, although probably slightly short in muzzle.

These two exquisitely "foxy" bitch heads exhibit remarkably similar proportions, but give slightly different impressions due to markings, coat color, and eye color. Both appear slightly short in muzzle in these photos. (Gene Merritt)

action. *Faults:* Chest too broad; "barrel ribs"; ribs too flat or weak.

Back: The back is straight and strong, with a level topline from withers to croup. It is of medium length, neither cobby nor slack from excessive length. The loin is taut and lean, narrower than the rib cage, and with a slight tuck-up. The croup slopes away from the spine at an angle, but never so steeply as to restrict the rearward thrust of the hind legs. *Faults:* Weak or slack back; roached back; sloping topline.

COMMENT: The neck is primarily what keeps a dog from falling on its face as the rear drives it forward. Muscles attached just below the base of the skull lift the forelimbs and propel them forward and back. The strength of these muscles is evident in the arched neck when the dog is alert and

Judging Siberians requires feeling carefully the size and shape of the rib cage and overall substance because coat can be deceiving. Note the difference in the appearance between the "new coat" phase (left) and "full coat" phase of the same quality bitch. (Jean Edwards & Joe C)

standing. But as they come into play in the moving dog, it becomes necessary for the head and neck to extend forward for maximum effectiveness. In the Siberian, we ask that the neck be medium in length simply because, like the medium skull, bone, etc., this is the most effective size where both speed and stamina are desirable.

The chest houses heart and lungs, and so should be of sufficient depth to provide ample room. But in a breed designed for maximum suppleness at a lope, the chest cannot be too wide, and must be flattened on the sides. Otherwise, it will impede the free movement of the front legs. So, too, with depth of chest. According to Roland

Lombard, there has probably never been an effective sled dog with a chest deeper than its elbows. In fact, in the well-built Siberian, it is probably only the hair on the chest that brings it to the level of the elbows, the chest itself being just higher and out of the way. Although the Standard asks for a "level topline," what is meant is the appearance of a level topline since, in fact, the spine dips downward from the withers above the shoulders before rising into the arch of the spine that creates the "tuck-up" in the loin. That arch is the main point of energy transference from the rear to the front, and in the effective galloper those muscles will be extremely powerful.

This winning brother/sister combination exhibits excellent type and proportions, as well as the typical structural differences between male and female. (Tatham)

Slightly overangulated in the rear, this bitch nevertheless has excellent proportions of height to length, length of leg to depth of chest, good shoulders, and excellent slope of croup and pelvis. (JoLynn Stresing)

TAIL

The well-furred tail of fox-brush shape is set on just below the level of the topline, and is usually carried over the back in a graceful sickle curve when the dog is at attention. When carried up, the tail does not curl to either side of the body, nor does it snap flat against the back. A trailing tail is normal for the dog when in repose. Hair on the tail is of medium length and approximately the same length on top, sides and bottom, giving the appearance of a round brush. *Faults:* A snapped or tightly curled tail; highly plumed tail; tail set too low or too high.

COMMENT: There are two elements that define the correct Siberian tail, the set and the carriage. The tail should be set on just below the level of the top line because of the slight fall away of the croup at about 30 to 35 degrees, but the carriage is of equal importance since it indicates much about the muscling of the rear assembly and the back. A correct tail may be carried in a relaxed sickle above the back when the dog is standing at attention or when it is moving, or it may be dropped when the animal is standing and trailing out behind when it is moving. But it should never touch the back or curl down the loin. When a Siberian is working, on the other hand, the tail is almost always trailing and may act as a kind of rudder that counterbalances movement to right or left. It is an interesting historical fact that so many early Siberians had fairly tight tails by current standards despite Leonhard Seppala's observation that the looser sickle tails worked better. I suspect that just as Arctic peoples tend to prefer dark dogs so as to instantly distinguish them from indigenous wolves, so, too, with the curled tail: It allowed them to distinguish at a glance whether the animal was lupine or canine. The request for the even brush shape rather than a heavily plumed tail is simply consistent with the medium-length coat that is requested in a section of the Standard which follows.

FOREQUARTERS

Shoulders: The shoulder blade is well laid back. The upper arm angles slightly backward from point of shoulder to elbow, and is never perpendicular to the ground. The muscles and ligaments holding the shoulder to the rib cage are firm and well developed. *Faults:* Straight shoulders; loose shoulders.

Forelegs: When standing and viewed from the front, the legs are moderately spaced, parallel and straight, with the elbows close to the body and turned neither in nor out. Viewed from the side, pasterns are slightly slanted, with the pastern joint strong, but flexible. Bone is substantial but never heavy. Length of the leg from elbow to ground is slightly more than the distance from the elbow to the top of withers. Dewclaws on forelegs may be removed. *Faults:* Weak pasterns; too heavy bone; too narrow or too wide in the front; out at the elbows.

Feet: Oval in shape but not long. The paws are medium in size, compact and well furred between the toes and pads. The pads are tough and thickly cushioned. The paws neither turn in nor out when the dog is in natural stance. *Faults:* Soft or splayed toes; paws too large and clumsy; paws too small and delicate; toeing in or out.

Excellent proportions on a very moderate, very balanced, very well-proportioned male, with good angle of upper arm, a strong topline, and nicely sloping croup. (John Ashbey)

COMMENT: In asking for a well laid back shoulder, I take the Standard to mean a shoulder blade that is angled approximately 30 to 40 degrees from the perpendicular, with 35 degrees being perhaps ideal. This, at least, is what studies of the racing sled dog have indicated. Though the benefits of extreme shoulder layback have long been touted by show ring "reach and drive" enthusiasts, Curtis Brown, in his book *Dog Locomotion and Gait Analysis,* is probably right when he suggests that extreme shoulder layback is probably only highly desirable in dogs meant to dig. This optimal angle of 35 degrees, then, is established when the heel pad is set directly under the center of the shoulder blade and not

Good proportion and type in a young male, especially the length and angle of upper arm and the length of muzzle (two characteristics which may be related). (Tom Nutting)

Apparently a bit straight in front and rear, this mature champion male nevertheless exhibits very good height to length proportions and a lovely head. (Mitchell)

when the feet are any further forward, as is sometimes the case in the show ring when the front is "dropped" into position by the handler. This is why it is also asked that the upper arm angle backward to the elbow and not be perpendicular to the ground, since a straight-shouldered dog can be made to give the appearance of having more shoulder layback by bringing the front legs forward, thus rotating the shoulder blade backward. The result, however, will be to bring the upper arm perpendicular to the ground. It is also true that contemporary show Siberians tend to have a shorter, straighter upper arm than is generally considered desirable.

But it is the muscles, tendons, and ligaments, and how they function, that are of paramount importance. Unfortunately, although it is implied, little is said about the lay-on or wraparound of the front assembly, which is absolutely crucial to a good front. But a front assembly is only as good as it functions, and it is while gaiting that a shoulder can be best appraised, according to its fluency, rotation of the blade (about 15 degrees according to Dr. Lombard), shock absorbency, and smoothness of topline. To the feel, good shoulders allow good muscling: the larger the blade, the larger the area for muscle adherence. And the smoother the blend of neck into topline, whether standing or gaiting, the better.

The front leg bones of the Siberian should be what is sometimes referred to as "bladed," that is to say, oval in shape (like the feet) and a bit sharp at the front edge. They are moderately (perhaps four fingers' to a palm's breadth) spaced for maximum efficiency. Pasterns are slanted slightly for maximum resiliency and flex, and the bone is moderate.

The Siberian's feet are his livelihood, and must be oval, strong, and definitely neither small nor round, however attractive judges sometimes find small cat feet. Small feet injure easily, and round feet with their shorter digits offer less flex and resiliency, and usually prefigure short, straight pasterns. And, of course, though dogs can certainly be set up in the show ring with their front toes pointing straight ahead, the more natural position for the feet on a well-built Siberian is with an approximate 10-degree toeing out. Otherwise, when the feet converge when moving, the strong middle toes do not land pointing straight ahead, so that one of the outer toes ends up taking the bulk of the stress.

HINDQUARTERS

When standing and viewed from the rear, the hind legs are moderately spaced and parallel. The upper thighs are well muscled and powerful, the stifles well bent, the hock joint well defined and set low to the ground. Dewclaws, if any, are to be removed. *Faults:* Straight stifles, cowhocks, too narrow or too wide in the rear.

COMMENT: This description of hindquarters is again in the interest of speed and endurance. The highest-hocked animals, like rabbits, run fastest but tire quickly. Short pasterns mean endurance. But though the Standard calls for a low hock joint, it is worth noting that Doc Lombard warns against a rear pastern that is too short, a hock joint that is too low, because too much speed is lost. In fact, a recent, fairly small sampling of measurements of working Siberians showed the length of the rear pasterns to be about one-third the height of the top of the pelvis in bitches and very slightly longer in males.

COAT

The coat of the Siberian Husky is double and medium in length, giving a well-furred appearance, but is never so long as to obscure the clean-cut outline of the dog. The undercoat is soft and dense and of sufficient length to support the outer coat. The guard hairs of the outer coat are straight and somewhat smooth lying, never harsh nor standing straight off from the body. It should be noted that the absence of the undercoat during the shedding season is normal. Trimming of whiskers and fur between the toes and around the feet to present a neater appearance is permissible. Trimming the fur on any other part of the dog is not to be condoned and should be severely penalized. *Faults:* Long, rough, or shaggy coat; texture too harsh or too silky; trimming of the coat, except as permitted above.

COMMENT: The Siberian Husky's coat is unique among Arctic breeds because of its medium length, both the Alaskan Malamute and the Samoyed having a somewhat longer, shaggier coat. The reason for this difference lies primarily in the difference in the climates in which these dogs were originally bred. In the case of the Siberian, the specific conditions of climate and terrain found in his homeland made the formation of ice balls in a long coat an ever-present danger. Thus, consciously or unconsciously, the Chukchi developed a coat on their dogs that could both withstand the Arctic cold and prevent the formation of ice balls. And it is for this reason that the long, shaggy, or coarse coat is specifically faulted by the Standard. Nevertheless, there does exist a certain range of coat length, probably from about 1 inch to 3 inches (varying somewhat on different areas of the body) that is considered typically Siberian so long as the dog's outline remains unobscured and the texture is correct. The love of profuse coat in the show fancy has led some breeders to produce coats so profuse as to require trimming of the underline to maintain a clean-cut outline. This is specifically prohibited by the Standard.

COLOR

All colors from black to pure white are allowed. A variety of markings on the head is common, including many striking patterns not found in other breeds.

COMMENT: One of the great delights of Siberians is their variability of color as well as markings and eye color—everything from all black to all white being both permissible and desirable. Usually symmetry is more aesthetically pleasing than asymmetry, but even so-called piebalds or pintos (though apparently not desirable to the Chukchi or many of the early breeders) are acceptable and occasionally even exquisite.

The great variety of colors and markings is part of the wide appeal of Siberians. Note the parti-colored eye on the black and white. (JoLynn Stresing)

GAIT

The Siberian Husky's characteristic gait is smooth and seemingly effortless. He is quick and light on his feet, and when in the show ring should be gaited on a loose lead at a moderately fast trot, exhibiting good

This old-fashioned "agouti" coloring sometimes throws judges in the ring, but it is a perfectly legitimate color variation, often accompanied by excellent pad pigmentation indicating tough foot pads. (Joe Asarisi)

reach in the forequarters and good drive in the hindquarters. When viewed from the front to rear while moving at a walk the Siberian Husky does not single-track, but as the speed increases the legs gradually angle inward until the pads are falling on a line directly under the longitudinal center of the body. As the pad marks converge, the forelegs and hind legs are carried straight forward, with neither elbows nor stifles turned in or out. Each hind leg moves in the path of the foreleg on the same side. While the dog is gaiting, the topline remains firm and level. *Faults:* Short, prancing or choppy gait, lumbering or rolling gait; crossing or crabbing.

COMMENT: With the exception of a few stipulations made in the interest of type and refinement, everything in the Standard so far has led up to this demand for "smooth and seemingly effortless" movement. In other words, this is where the phrase "the whole equals the sum of the parts" is particularly relevant, since, basically, the moving dog is the whole dog. Consequently, a dog that exhibits a well-bent stifle but a somewhat steep shoulder while standing is also likely to show this discrepancy when moving. Balance is the key to movement, in other words, and a dog who is slightly underangulated, but balanced, front and rear, will probably move better than, and is thus preferable to, a dog who is extreme in one quarter but not the other. It should be noted, too, that any forward reach that plants the foot any further forward than directly under the ear or eye is inefficient as it creates negative energy by essentially putting on the brakes every time the foot hits the ground. Positive, forward energy only happens after the front leg becomes perpendicular to the body. The request for single-tracking and for the rear legs to follow in the line of the front is in the interest of efficiency. A dog who is more angulated in the rear than in the front, for instance, is likely to crab, especially if he has a short, stiff back. In other words, he will tend to move diagonally to the line of travel, placing his rear feet to one side or the other of his forefeet in order to avoid actually hitting his front feet with his rear feet. Insufficient angulation or straight pasterns usually cause short, prancing, or choppy gaits. Since this construction causes the dog to bob up and down rather than

Two significant champions in the author's breeding program showing approximately equivalent body proportions on a dog and a bitch. Both appear athletic, showing good length of leg in proportion to depth of chest. Both, however, are probably slightly long in body; he having a slightly sloping topline, and she a somewhat flat croup. (Stephen Klein / Janet Ashbey)

move directly in the line of travel, he is apt to be slower and tire more quickly. A lumbering or rolling gait is caused by a dog's inability to track properly, either because of an inherited weakness in structure or poor muscle tone. Often, overweight dogs exhibit this tendency, and puppies often tend to roll somewhat before they achieve adequate muscular development and coordination. Since this type of movement also produces motion in a direction outside the line of travel, it is less than efficient. The same is true of any movement of the legs other than directly forward to a point directly under the longitudinal center of the body.

Occasionally the comment is heard at ringside, "That dog looks like he could pull a sled." Too often this comment is made in reference to a heavily boned, heavily muscled dog who, when simply being gaited, already looks like he is pulling a 200-pound load. Remember that the Standard asks for a balance of power, speed, and endurance, and that this balance will be reflected in a dog who is "light and quick on his feet" and whose "gait is smooth and seemingly effortless."

TEMPERAMENT

The characteristic temperament of the Siberian Husky is friendly and gentle, but also alert and outgoing. He does not display the possessive qualities of the guard dog, nor is he overly suspicious of strangers

Absolutely beautiful body proportions, angles, and head planes are evident on this old-fashioned "dark dog" that comes down from Dr. Roland Lombard's famous Igloo Pak racing lines.

or aggressive with other dogs. Some measure of reserve and dignity may be expected in the mature dog. His intelligence, tractability, and eager disposition make him an agreeable companion and willing worker.

COMMENT: Temperament is of the utmost importance in a Siberian Husky. An aggressive dog is not a team dog, and since the Siberian is a sled dog, any sign of aggression toward other dogs should be severely penalized. Shyness is equally undesirable, though somewhat more historically rooted.

SUMMARY

The most important breed characteristics of the Siberian Husky are medium size, moderate bone, well-balanced proportions, ease and freedom of movement, proper coat, pleasing head and ears, correct tail, and good disposition. Any appearance of excessive bone or weight, constricted or clumsy gait, or long, rough coat should be penalized. The Siberian Husky never appears so heavy or coarse as to suggest a freighting animal; nor is he so light and fragile as to suggest a sprint-racing animal. In both sexes the Siberian Husky gives the appearance of being capable of great endurance. In addition to the faults already noted, the obvious structural faults common to all breeds are as undesirable in the Siberian Husky as in any other breed, even though they are not specifically mentioned herein.

COMMENT: While I believe this summary is really a perfect summation of the breed in the context of a Standard, I'd like to broaden the perspective slightly and suggest that first and foremost the Siberian is a distance galloper and needs longer leg than depth of chest, only slightly more length of body than height, a short loin, long sloping croup and shoulders. In short, there is nothing husky about a Husky (which is merely a corruption of the word "esky" for Eskimo). His is more a wiry, endurance strength than a heavily muscled one. He exhibits the nimble quickness of a shortstop or tennis player, not the brute strength of the football player. So even though a very full coat may give him a rich plushness in appearance, he is a lean, hard dog underneath: a Bruce Jenner, for instance, or a Martina Navratilova—certainly not a John Elway or a Barry Saunders, but maybe a Deion Sanders.

(Winter Churchill Photography)

CHAPTER 4

Finding the Right Siberian—Puppy, Adult, or Rescue

Assuming you have decided to acquire a Siberian Husky—there are several conditions you will have to accept going in. Know that you will need a very secure run or fenced-in yard, an inexhaustible supply of patience, and more than a little cunning to match that of your newest family member. This "noble savage" will come genetically compelled to "push the envelope" in ways you may have never imagined. You must now decide: Will you seek a puppy, adult, or rescue dog? Everyone believes, of course, that they want a cuddly 8-week-old puppy; and Siberian puppies are, in fact, just about the most adorable 8-week-old animals on the face of the earth. They really are like living teddy bears, and who could resist a teddy bear? BUT there are compelling reasons to carefully weigh your options and consider the possible outcome of your decision.

As with all dogs, Siberian Husky temperament is in a very large sense a matter of the individual dog's genes. And, as with all dogs, 8-week-old puppies are pretty much "hard-wired" into what they are going to be as adults. So knowing your puppy's genetic background and the environment in which she spent her first eight weeks are the most crucial predictive elements in anticipating disposition and temperament. That, then, is the strongest argument for acquiring a dog from a highly reputable, very experienced breeder: There is simply no substitute. If you take this crucial, wise first step, everything else becomes easier.

At this breeder's facility, you may find lots of dog hair, certain odors that after, say, six house-reared litters, has permeated some secret core of the house that no deep cleaning, short of a flame-thrower, could possibly penetrate (at least that's often true at my house. Avoid all breeders with all-white living rooms; they're obviously schizophren-ics!). But you will also find dogs with lots of exercise room, clean (though not necessarily slick) whelping facilities, and you will have the general sense that the dogs, while perhaps living a more rugged, outdoorsy life than the average house pet, are leading happy, healthy lives, and are simply delighted to have you visit. You will notice, in short, that the lives of the dogs are obviously quite central to the life of the household, though the sizes of breeding kennels vary considerably.

You, of course, will have lots of questions. Perhaps to your surprise, so will the breeder: How large is your secured area, and is it escape-proof? How many hours will the animal be left home alone? How old are your children? You will feel more like you've come to an adoption agency than to a car lot—with makes, models, and price break-downs. Typically, the inventory is not large.

Sibes in synch: a pair of Bill and Lois Leonard's Willo Siberians trying for a "photo finish."

THE PUPPY CHOICE

If you choose a young puppy in such a situation, you have the advantage of meeting its parents, usu-ally, and having a good idea of how that puppy has been raised. With the help of the breeder, you can probably find the right puppy for your needs, and, again with the help of the breeder, raise that puppy into a happy, well-adjusted, good citizen. But, like children, Siberians start out without any manners: They must be housetrained, taught not to use their mouths on people, not to chew electrical cords and Persian carpets, to sleep past 3 A.M., to walk on a lead without pulling your arm out of its socket, and generally be given a great deal of direc-tion. Often, first-time Siberian owners, especially those with busy schedules, are simply not up to the task, and their cute 8-week-old puppy turns into a 50- or 60-pound "wild child" with the strength of a bull and the willfulness of a pampered prince or princess. And that's when the not-so-cute young adult often goes back to the breeder or to the humane shelter or to some unsuspecting neighbor with a soft heart.

THE ADULT CHOICE

The alternative is either an older puppy, a young adult, or even an older dog. The advantage here is that you take some-

To live is to run: A youngster finds its legs. (Cheryl Scheall)

thing home that is already trained or partially trained, and that will take much less energy to make into a credit to your household. The reason most people want a puppy, or believe they want a puppy, is that they believe it will grow up to be "more truly theirs." While this may be true of some breeds, it is generally not true of Siberians. In fact, for a myriad of psycho-social reasons too numerous to list here, the adult or young adult may bond with you more quickly than a puppy and develop into a more loyal companion. Many reputable breeders will often have young adults available that may have fallen a little short of their show or working expectations, but are excellent candidates as pets nonetheless, and may be had for a somewhat lower price. The same is true of dogs retired from

the show ring or the breeding program who still have many good years of love and loyalty to offer. Siberians typically live thirteen to seventeen years, though they are vulnerable to cancers and the like from about ten years onward. So sometimes the 6- or 7-year-old ex-brood bitch makes a wonderful house pet, especially for older people who value the relative calmness of these animals.

Six-foot-high fencing is highly recommended for a dog yard intended to accommodate a Siberian Husky.

A golden girl basking in golden sun—one of the lighter shades of the so-called "red" color phase. (JoLynn Stresing)

THE RESCUE OPTION

But if you're the sort of person who would like to help a good dog out of a bad situation, the rescue programs sponsored and coordinated by the Siberian Husky Club of America may be the best option of all. While it is true, according to veterinarian Bruce Fogle in his book, *The Dog's Mind: Understanding Your Dog's Behavior* (New York: Howell Book House, 1990), that 80 percent of serious dog bites are inflicted by animals from pounds, and who may have missed important developmental elements in their puppyhood; it is equally true that Siberian temperament and disposition are pretty easily deciphered in body language by any breed expert, and all animals in rescue operations associated with the Siberian Husky Club of America will have been screened by just such experts.

(Winter Churchill Photography)

CHAPTER 5

Living with a Siberian Husky

PREPARING THE NEW HOME

Before bringing your new Siberian home, you should have an exercise area secured by a fence that measures at least 5 feet high, preferably higher, that is either dig-proof with a foot or so buried underground or complemented by a smaller dog run that is similarly dig-proof. You should have a dog crate of an appropriate size—about 24 inches high by 36 inches long for the adult Siberian, which the puppy can grow into. Most crates are made in two basic styles—wire mesh and more enclosed plastic or molded fiberglass. The latter weigh less and are approved for airline travel. The wire crate allows the dog more visibility, better air circulation, and is collapsible. It's really a personal choice, but the better models of both styles are most easily and economically acquired through various wholesale catalogs that most dog breeders have by the wagonload. These catalogs are also the best sources for leashes, collars, food bowls, chew toys, and the like, which your breeder can advise you about. The person who sells you your

Barrels are a venerable tradition in Siberian housing. (Gene Merritt)

puppy can also give you a copy of one of the catalogs! These supplies are also available at well-stocked pet stores. If there is one near you and you don't want to have your equipment shipped, you might want to visit the shop to see what is available.

GUIDANCE IN A NUTSHELL

What follows is a series of puppy-rearing tips I furnish to anyone acquiring a Siberian from me, plus a more in-depth analysis of the process. Written by Denis Ferentinos and Mary Ferentino, it was created as part of the pamphlet, *A Partnership For Life/Learning to Understand Your Siberian,* published by the Siberian Husky Club of America. Though the focus is on puppy rearing, most of the principles apply in varying degrees to the older dog as well.

YOUR NEW PUPPY

The first days and nights with your new puppy are often the hardest. The puppy has been sharing the collective heartbeat of the litter. In their birth home, puppies wake up together, play together, sleep together (often on top of each other), try out their first growls, barks, and feats of tussling strength on each other. So when your puppy comes to you, he will understandably be a little lost and confused. There is no doubt he will relish the special attention you will give him, but (especially at night) there will be times when he misses his brothers and sisters. As hard as this transition period can be, however, you can use it to your advantage.

Bonding

Feeling a little insecure in new surroundings (sounds, smells, schedules, people), new puppies experience a strong need to bond with their new pack—you. So crate the puppy near where you sleep, if at all possible, so you can reassure him during his first night or two. Put old clothes you have worn in the crate, so the puppy finds comfort in your particular scent and takes it to be the olfactory signature of his new family. If the puppy must be left alone, leave a radio or TV on for him as comfort noise, and never leave him alone outside a crate or a restricted area. Make doubly certain that he cannot get near electrical cords, houseplants, insulation, or any potentially toxic substances—puppies, like babies, want to put everything in their mouths.

Give the Puppy Plenty of Sleeping Opportunities

Puppies typically sleep most of the time. My young puppies sleep two and half hours to every half hour they're up playing or eating. And they really need that much sleep to stay happy and healthy. So, even though it's especially hard on the kids in a family who are anxious to play with a new puppy, it's very important to let the puppy have plenty of "down time" in the early weeks.

The lure of the great outdoors: a 4-month-old puppy looking "wolfishly" alert. (JoLynn Stresing)

Housetraining

Use a crate. It may take your new puppy several days to get used to his crate. During this time, he may scream bloody murder about being confined, but stick with it, and never let him out in response to his protests. The only exception is when it's first thing in the morning when *he really has to go*. Otherwise, either ignore the screaming, or slap the crate with a "no" command, or use a water pistol, until the puppy accepts his crate time. Then, always take the puppy outside as soon as he comes out of the crate and before putting him back in. If the puppy does have an accident in the house, pick him up immediately, and even a little abruptly, with a "no" command, and then take him outside. Do this, however, *only when you see the puppy have the accident and never reprimand him after the fact;* he simply won't understand. And always *praise* the puppy when he uses the appropriate spot.

Playing

Puppies normally play rough among themselves, but they have thick coats and tough skins. You don't. So teaching a puppy not to use his mouth when playing with people is extremely important. From the time the puppy walks into your house, *everyone* who has any contact with him should always discourage biting. Small taps across the muzzle with a "no biting" or "no" command should be sufficient to send the message, if done consistently over time. *No one should play roughly with the puppy,* encouraging him to use his mouth. Ripped clothes and. inevitably, punctured skin will result, and the puppy will get blamed. And it's all so avoidable with good training.

Feeding

Puppies require three to four feedings a day till they reach 6 months of age, two feedings from 6 months to 1 year, and then one or two feedings a day thereafter. Necessary intake varies from puppy to puppy and with age, activity, and season. Typically, total daily intake will range from as much as four or even five cups a day in the rapidly growing 4- to 7-month-old puppy to as little as two cups or less in the older animal. It is more

A great deal of wonderful research has gone into the development of modern dog foods and feeding methods. Be sure to ask your puppy's breeder for a printed diet and a small supply of the food your new puppy has been eating. (Winter Churchill Photography)

important to pay close attention to the look and feel of your dog: He is too fat when you can't feel individual ribs and his waist is thick and soft; too thin is when backbone and hip bones are too prominent and waist is too drawn. Generally, it's better for a puppy to be a little lean than a little chubby; and it's typical for adolescents and yearlings to be a bit thin and gawky. Kennel dogs often overeat, if given a chance, while single pets often become picky eaters as a way to manipulate their owners. *Always put food down for no more than ten minutes.* If the puppy does not eat it, pick it up until the next scheduled feeding. Do not add other goodies to the food or you will be bringing him home steak before you know it. The best dog foods for Siberians are high-energy, high-performance foods not usually available in supermarkets, but often available through feed stores. They usually approach 30 percent protein and sometimes as much as 20 percent fat. Siberians do not seem to tolerate the high cereal content of most commercial dog foods and will develop loose stools when these are fed.

The Siberian Husky puppy going into a new home should be bursting with health and mirror his well-being throughout. (Winter Churchill Photography)

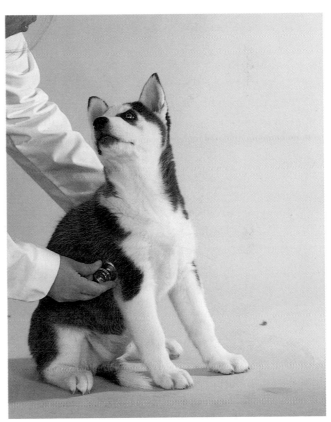

It is in the interest of your puppy's breeder, yourself and, most of all, your new puppy, that he be thoroughly checked by a veterinarian as soon as possible after you get him. (Winter Churchill Photography)

Health

Your puppy should be guaranteed to be in good health the day you get him, but a trip to your vet with a stool sample is strongly recommended within the first week, and it is very important to keep track of the various shots your puppy will need during the first sixteen weeks and yearly thereafter. Typically, puppies should not get respiratory colds like people do, and any such symptoms should quickly be seen by your vet. Occasional loose stools, on the other hand, are quite typical of puppies, especially if they find an open food bag or eat something they shouldn't, and sometimes a day on rice, boiled hamburger or chicken, and burnt (really burnt) toast is all it takes to settle an irritated bowel (along with a little over-the-counter diarrhea remedy). But any blood or foul smell associated with the stool is reason to get to the vet immediately. Dehydration debilitates puppies quickly and is therefore extremely dangerous.

Be the Boss

Puppies need guidance to become good citizens, and your puppy is genetically programmed to accept the hierarchy of the pack. So everyone involved with him must be prepared to take a leadership role in his eyes.

Consistency, firmness, and patience are the keys to doing this. All established rules should be agreed upon by all members of the family: when and where can the puppy go, on the couch or off, on the bed or off, what can be chewed, etc. And then everyone must abide by the same rules or the

"Lounge Lizard." (Sue Shane)

puppy will become confused. Much good training can be reinforced with treats, should always be reinforced with lots of praise, and no training should ever take place when the trainer is feeling impatient or short-tempered. A basic obedience course or puppy kindergarten course typically offered by local dog clubs is strongly recommended. If your young puppy seems to be acting particularly headstrong, roll him on his back and scratch his tummy until he goes relaxed and becomes passive. By doing this, you insist on his showing a submissive attitude, but at the same time you offer a pleasant alternative (having his tummy scratched, which almost all Siberians love) to taking charge. You remain the boss, but the puppy gets something in exchange. And everyone in the family should scratch the puppy's chest just as a friendly gesture. One should also always try to keep kids from getting a puppy too revved up and excited; someone ends up getting scratched or nipped and the puppy doesn't understand what he did wrong. I have a friend who raised her children with the understanding: Anyone who gets bitten gets spanked. No one was ever bitten, or spanked.

Be Intuitive

Rules can only take you so far in caring for and training a puppy; often you must rely on gut intuition. Trust yourself. After several weeks or months of getting into your puppy's head, you'll know that puppy better than anyone. You'll know whether he's really sick or just a little under the weather. You'll know whether a certain desired behavior is being resisted or simply being misunderstood. The examples are numerous.

Have Fun

I think we often learn more from animals than they ever learn from us. And one of the great

"Tough Love": Adults at play. (Gene Merritt)

pleasures that I've always gotten from Siberians is simply in watching them be themselves: the natural grace and agility, the self-confidence, the predatory alertness alternating with clownish cuddliness. And there are few pleasures greater, I think, than having a long relationship with a truly great animal. "Dogs have short lives," Mark Twain said—"perhaps their only fault." Your dog's life will be largely what you make it; the point of good training is that you'll both enjoy that life and one another more fully.

from A PARTNERSHIP FOR LIFE: Learning to Understand your Siberian Husky, *by Denis Ferentinos and Mary Ferentino.*

DON'T BLAME THE DOG!

Little did our Stone Age ancestors realize, when they first invited the wolves in their environment

In a home with a Siberian Husky puppy, family members soon learn to shut the refrigerator door—firmly! (Winter Churchill Photography)

into the family of man, that what they had begun was a symbiotic relationship unlike any other in the history of human society.

Humans have shared their homes, their food, and their everyday lives with dogs for thousands of years. We've manipulated their gene pools to such an extent as to make some breeds appear as nearly separate species while others remain almost indistinguishable from their lupine ancestors. We employ them for sport, amusement, recreation, work, and even for saving us from ourselves. In return, we willingly feed them, groom them, heal them, bathe them, and lavish our deepest affection upon them.

But what we most need to do for them is often overlooked. Mostly we need to try understanding them, and appreciate them for what they truly are—dogs, animals who think, react, and respond in ways that are entirely alien to us.

They perceive the world in ways far different than we ever will, living by senses we have either lost or will never attain. They are not small, furry people—they are dogs, with a history, a pride, and a dignity unique unto themselves.

Inviting a Siberian Husky into your household requires *you* to accept the responsibility for the creation of a mutually beneficial relationship, one built on trust, respect, and sensitivity. Establishing such a partnership successfully means understanding your dog's needs rather than merely imposing your will on a subordinate.

So, when your puppy howls, don't blame the dog. When your puppy digs or chews or barks or whines, don't blame the dog. Your puppy is only doing the one thing he knows best—being a dog. The role of the truly responsible Siberian Husky owner includes accepting the varying manifestations of your Siberian's genetic predisposition at face value, and learning the most advantageous ways of dealing with them. Learn to appreciate Siberians for the magical creatures they are, instead of the fictional creatures we sometimes would like them to be.

Whether your puppy's future holds a place in the breed, Obedience, or Agility ring, a spot on a sled team, or the full-time job of beloved family member, the need for understanding and enlightenment remains first and foremost. Most importantly, we sincerely hope that the information that follows will help you to gain a broader perspective and a new way of seeing: an opportunity to look at the world through dog-colored glasses.

Five-month-old puppies are joyously eager for anything! (JoLynn Stresing)

How Dogs Learn

Despite what you may think, the majority of what your Siberian learns doesn't take place at the end of a leash. Active learning is taking place every moment your dog is involved in some form

A friend is where you find one. (Cheryl Scheall)

of interaction with you, your family, friends, other dogs, and the overall environment and has been going on since the moment your dog was born.

The process by which a dog learns is deceptively simple and straightforward, resulting from the way he perceives the world: Every action generates a reaction, and every reaction can be categorized as either pleasant or unpleasant. For dogs, there are none of the "middle grounds" or "gray areas" that so often complicate human decision-making.

Actions which result in something pleasant, such as food, praise, petting, play, or the satisfying of any other instinctive need, are more likely to be repeated. Actions which result in something which the dog perceives as unpleasant, such as a check on the collar, a harsh tone of voice, or physical discomfort, are less likely to be repeated. A classic example is the dog who jumps up on the kitchen counter. If the action results in the dog obtaining a morsel of food, anything placed on that counter

A head study among the peonies. (JoLynn Stresing)

will become fair game. If, on the other hand, the act of jumping up results in the dog's paw landing on a hot burner, your dog will have learned something else entirely. In either case, an immediately memorable learning experience has taken place without any participation on your part whatsoever.

Once people enter the equation, however, the process becomes somewhat more complex. Part of accepting responsibility for the well-being of a creature constantly engaged in some form of learning means accepting the need to be constantly engaged in the act of teaching. While dogs will instinctively adapt to their own environment, they can only adapt to our society with our active participation. We must assume the responsibility for providing the positive and negative reactions to their behavior that will allow them to understand how life works in our world. We become responsible for teaching them the behaviors that nature couldn't be expected to furnish. The

ability to teach depends upon the skill to communicate effectively, which, in turn, involves three basic requirements: immediacy, consistency, and validity.

Immediacy

Siberian Huskies are very nearly "Zen-like" in their approach to life. They exist, they "are," they live in the "now." Dogs learn in the present, while either thought or the action is actually occurring. This is the only time when dogs can make the vital connection between a particular action and the ensuing result. Once the action has been completed, the dog is incapable of thinking back and making the kind of abstract cause-and-effect leap of logic required to link past and present.

This also applies to threats or promises of future rewards. Promises, such as, "If you do that again, you're really gonna get it," or, "If you behave while I'm gone, I'll give you a treat when I return," are useless. Even if your dog was capable of clearly understanding the words, the intent itself would remain meaningless.

Studies have shown that for a positive reinforcement to be truly effective, it must be given within *one second* of the desired action. The same time frame can also be applied to the act of extinguishing undesirable behavior.

Consistency

One of the things that makes learning math possible for us is consistency; two plus two always equals four. Imagine how difficult learning even basic addition would be, however, if the answer was occasionally different. Confusion would lead to frustration, and eventually to an utter disinterest in learning math at all. Learning takes place in the shortest period of time with the highest retention when the information is absolute. Basic spelling doesn't become a real problem until you're faced with things like "I before E except after C." It's the gray areas that slow the process down.

If you allow your dog on the couch while watching your favorite television programs on Tuesday, you can't expect him to stay "off" that same couch just because you have company on Saturday. If your behavior is inconsistent, it's a safe bet that your dog's will be, as well.

Validity

Fairness, kindness, and sensitivity are integral parts of our interaction with our dogs. While there's no question that you could train your dog not to jump up on you by beating him severely whenever he did it, your overreaction would hardly help establish a loving relationship between the two of you. While you may succeed in stopping him from jumping up, you will definitely have taught him that something quite unpleasant occurs whenever he tries to greet you and act friendly. Simply teaching your dog that he must sit to be petted not only replaces the undesirable behavior with a desirable one, it also strengthens the bond you have with him. We have at our command a variety of means for expressing our displeasure with our dogs' behavior, some more physical than others. From a cold stare to a harsh word, a shake on the scruff of the neck, or a check

The old-fashioned "agouti" or dark-faced phase, shown in the puppy at the left, can be a lovely variation. (Joe Asarisi)

on the collar, the most valid choice is the one that requires the *least* amount of physical force necessary to achieve the desired response. The idea is to communicate, not intimidate.

Simply put, Siberian Huskies, like humans, want to know "what's in it for me?" A happy, confident Siberian with an eager-to-please attitude will only result from being given the opportunity to learn in an enriched environment where learning is a predominantly enjoyable experience. When accomplishments are applauded and communication is clear, learning can become a rich and rewarding process.

PACK STRUCTURE

Dogs, as descendants of wolves, are pack animals. In order for wolves to hunt successfully, a highly organized social structure was necessary. Survival required hunting, hunting required coordination, and coordination depended upon a capable leader. The animal that you've brought into your home may no longer need to bring down a caribou for his dinner, but the need for a strong sense of pack identity is as much a part of your Siberian's genetic programming today as it was thousands of years ago.

Pack structure goes far beyond the need for food, however; it permeates the entire life of each individual Siberian to such a degree that it allows them to assume roles in our own families, even though we are an entirely different species. This powerful requirement for a sense of belonging to a pack or family stems from the fact that dogs, like wolves, are highly social, gregarious animals. Like the need for food, a Siberian's need for companionship is virtually primal in nature; it is a part of the breed's very makeup, and a serious part indeed. A Siberian's need for a sense of pack structure and leadership is a survival instinct. As a result, a Siberian's place in his pack is not a casual consideration; it is a situation that is constantly tested and evaluated.

The instinctual need to belong to a pack, however, doesn't end upon simply gaining acceptance. From the moment you bring a Siberian into your home, you and every other member of your household become your dog's new pack. Since every pack must have a leader, and every

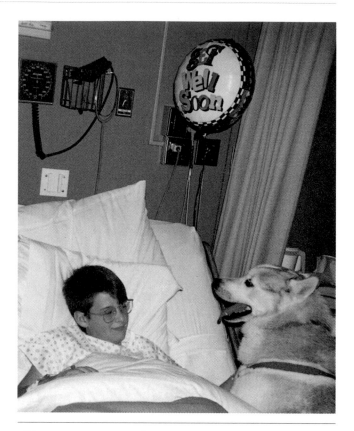

Siberians are in great demand as Therapy dogs in hospitals and nursing homes.

dog has the innate ability to fill that position, should the dog perceive it necessary to do so, it's up to *you* to define the new pack order. The essential ingredient in a happy and successful relationship with your Siberian is both simple and categorical: You must *establish yourself* as the undisputed leader of the pack.

Good leadership is a rather complex issue, involving the combination of two important skills: the ability to communicate clearly and the patience to act with consistency. The benevolent leader gains respect by dispensing discipline quickly and firmly only when it is necessary, every time it's called for, and always in a fair and sensitive manner.

The leader of any pack—human, dog, or wolf—exhibits these attributes at all times. Failure to establish yourself as pack leader will leave your dog no choice but to assume that role, with some dogs rising to the task more eagerly than others. The only truly successful long-term relationship is the one in which the owner is the leader, since it is ultimately the responsibility of the owner to make the decisions which will affect the safety and well-being of the dog and the overall harmony of the household. At some point in our lives, we've all had a chance to see dogs who've risen to the role of leader of their pack. The overt signs are easy to identify: Dogs who growl at or bite their owners, who won't come when they're called, or who drag their owners around by their leashes are all making their perception of the pack structure quite clear.

Put yourself in your dog's position for a moment. We essentially wait on them hand and foot, providing clean bedding, good food, fresh water, toys, and attention, with little or no effort expected from them. They go out when they want to, have someone to play with, and quickly discover that they're quicker, faster, and quite often stronger than we can ever hope to be. Unless you indicate otherwise, what conclusion could your dog possibly reach about who's in charge?

While leadership is a function of dominance, Siberians establish dominance in ways that are sometimes a great deal more subtle than you might expect. Establishing yourself as the dominant

A Siberian's body language is highly expressive, especially through tails and ears. (JoLynn Stresing)

member of the pack can be done with equal subtlety, rarely, if ever, requiring brute physical force. Good leadership is benign, borne out of continuing respect rather than random violence. Don't set a precedent of aggression as the means for becoming dominant. The successful pack leader leads through example and retains the position by gaining the respect of the other pack members. Self-assuredness, confidence, authority, intelligence, and dignity are the attributes expected of a leader.

One of the most effective means of establishing leadership is by assuming the role that the older, more senior members of the wolf pack play with the younger members—that of teacher. Enrolling your puppy in a structured training class utilizing a positive reinforcement method of teaching will help circumvent some of the ways in which dogs display dominance. Pulling on their leashes, pushing past their owners to go out a door, stealing food from the table, refusing to stand still to be groomed or examined by the veterinarian, or generally ignoring commands are all examples of how dogs constantly test to see who is really in charge.

Training goes beyond the act of establishing proper responses to commands, however. It helps create an environment in which you as pack leader can either grant or deny permission for any number of activities. Equally as important, training creates situations in which your dog can gain your approval, whether through petting, giving treats, or sincere verbal praise, in a manner that is directly linked to his actions.

Petting your dog automatically every time he nudges your hand is often an entirely unconscious act, but one which is full of meaning to your dog. Insisting that your dog respond to a command such as "sit" in order to earn that scratch behind the ears puts you in the leadership role. A game of "tug-of-war" can be just as enlightening. Allowing your dog to end up with the toy should always be your decision, never your dog's.

As in housetraining and stress management, maintaining a routine can also be a useful tool in promoting a clear pack order. By simply complying with your dog's wishes any time he wants to go out, wants a treat or a toy, you are unintentionally granting your dog the position of dominant decision maker. Set a routine that you can both live with, and do your best to adhere to that routine.

Above all, once having earned your Siberian's respect, work hard at maintaining it through sensitive leadership and a true sense of partnership. Taking the time to lay the groundwork for a strong relationship when your Siberian is young will bring you many rewards as your lives continue together.

SOCIALIZATION

Imagine a parent who believes that the correct way to raise a child is to isolate that child from any and all outside influences. Accordingly, there is no exposure to other children or adults, no rides in a

An Iditarod competitor at play. (Joe Asarisi)

car except for trips to the doctor or dentist, and a world that consists of nothing more than their own house and yard. Now try to imagine what that child's first day of school would be like, with bus rides, noisy hallways, bells ringing, strange children and teachers, and the inability to assimilate any of it. Within a very short period of time, the child would more than likely either curl up in a corner and tremble, or turn into an uncontrollable frenzy of activity.

Obviously, no rational person would knowingly raise a child that way, yet people unwittingly subject their dogs to similar situations every day, purely as a result of improperly socializing them as puppies. While puppies are certainly not children, the responsibilities for developing a young mind to its fullest potential remain very much the same.

Socialization is a term used to describe the process of exposing puppies to the widest variety of stimuli and experiences at the earliest possible age in an effort to promote their development into confident, outgoing, well-adjusted adolescents and adults. Undersocialized dogs abound in today's society, dogs who appear normal, healthy, and happy in the living room with the family, but who bark at every noise or visitor, snarl at every passing dog, and do everything in their power to avoid the inside of a car.

With just a little forethought and a nominal amount of effort, many of these problem behaviors can be prevented. Here's a few suggestions for a socialization program that will require a little of your time now, but will make life with your Siberian a great deal more pleasant in the future.

Siberians love just about everyone, even cats if they've been raised with them. (Sue Shane)

For many dogs, their only rides in a car end up at a vet's office, trips that are usually stressful and occasionally unpleasant, and therefore generally memorable for all the wrong reasons. Taking your puppy for rides of increasing duration will prevent a negative association, as well as gradually overcoming any tendencies toward motion sickness.

Opening your doors to friends, family, and anyone else you can invite over will allow your puppy to meet lots of strangers in a familiar place. And since you'll both be in the car so much anyway, you can give those trips a purpose by taking the puppy to meet people in unfamiliar places, too.

Once your puppy is fully immunized to infectious diseases and is used to a collar and leash, visits to public parks, playgrounds, the beach, shopping centers, and busy sidewalks will provide exposure not only to people of all ages, sizes, and shapes, but a vast array of different settings as well. It's important to start slowly, however. A 9-week-old puppy may find the biggest shopping mall in the county a little too much culture shock. Encourage people to gently pet your puppy, but be careful not to let them become too overwhelming. Suggest that receptive people crouch down, and let the puppy initiate the contact by coming up to *them*. The idea is for the dog to become comfortable with strangers, not frightened or intimidated by them.

A puppy that grows up as the only dog in a household may be thoroughly at ease with people, but gravely lacking in the social skills necessary to interact with other dogs. While one answer would be to acquire many dogs in the name of canine emotional well-being, this is probably not be a workable solution for everyone.

A more practical approach is to use the same methods for dog-socializing your Siberian as you do for people-socializing. Invite responsible friends to bring their reliable, well-behaved dogs over for a visit, then arrange to visit them in return. Look for parks and similar places where other dog owners congregate.

Puppy kindergartens and training classes for young dogs are usually available through commercial training centers, local dog training clubs and 4-H groups. If you're planning on showing your dog in either conformation or Obedience Trials, start bringing your puppy to local matches. Getting puppies accustomed to the routine of attending

dog shows and all the activity associated with the typical show environment will result in a dog that will be much more relaxed when it comes time to launch their own show careers.

A dog who leaves the company of other dogs behind entirely at the age of 7 or 8 weeks misses the opportunity to develop the language and nuances of intraspecies communication. Dogs such as these are much more likely to become what is known as "dog aggressive," and may remain unable to socialize with other dogs whatsoever for the remainder of their lives.

The most important pitfall to avoid is the inadvertent reinforcement of antisocial behavior. When your puppy barks and growls at a stranger, it's a natural reaction to attempt to calm the puppy through petting and using a soothing tone of voice. Unfortunately, what we intend as reassurance can be interpreted entirely differently by the puppy, who may see your actions as approval for his defensive (offensive) behavior. The proper time for praise and reassurance is at the moment your puppy is behaving in a manner of which you approve. Encourage your puppy to be curious, imaginative, intrepid, and willing to attempt new things.

It is infinitely preferable to reward your puppy for acting friendly and handling new situations with a positive and forthright attitude than to reward for overtly antisocial behavior. Fostering a confident, well-adjusted, outgoing Siberian is a responsibility which lies solely with a responsible owner, and one that begins with the first day you bring your puppy home. The rewards you will both gain through a conscientious program of

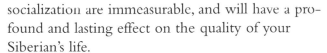

Daughter and dad: A sensitive portrait in winter twilight. (JoLynn Stresing)

The heavier the snow, the happier the Siberian. (Cheryl Scheall)

socialization are immeasurable, and will have a profound and lasting effect on the quality of your Siberian's life.

The essence of good socialization is based upon providing a truly enriched environment for your puppy. A Siberian who is exposed to an assortment of experiences as a puppy will have the opportunity to mature into an adult who can confidently face life's challenges and surprises while taking them all in stride.

STRESS

As you look at your Siberian puppy napping peacefully at the foot of your bed or playing contentedly with a chew toy, it's easy to envy him. He has food and water delivered to him, a family who loves him, no bills to pay, or lunatic drivers to cut him off on the freeway—he's the embodiment of the old cliché, "a dog's life."

To the untrained eye, his life seems far more peaceful and serene than our own; quite nearly idyllic.

The truth of the matter is that stress plays as important a role in your Siberian's day-to-day life as it does in yours, with just as profound an impact. Even the root causes of the stress itself are similar. Anxiety, the fear of pain, an unexpected change in his normal routine, or just an unpalatable meal can be as stressful to your dog as they can be to you.

As in humans, the entire gamut of stress-related behavior in dogs is highly individualized, dependent upon both genetics and environment. Different dogs will react in entirely different ways to similar situations, and, furthermore, will exhibit stress to varying degrees by different means. While it is no more possible to create a stress-free environment for our dogs than it is to create one for ourselves, we do have the ability to refrain from unintentionally adding more stress as a result of ignoring or misunderstanding our dogs' needs.

The first step toward achieving this goal is to learn to recognize the ways in which stress manifests itself in dogs. From a purely physiological point of view, there are certain signs which are common among all types of dogs, such as panting, licking, dilated pupils, sweaty paws, and runny noses. In terms of the behavioral manifestations, however, dogs generally fall into one of two categories: positive stressors and negative stressors, and much of what you may currently be misinterpreting as misbehavior is actually stress-related behavior.

Positive stressing is relatively easy to identify. A dog who is prone to bursts of barking, whining, pacing, shredding, or chewing is probably a positive stressor.

Negative stressing is quite a bit less obvious. As opposed to the positive stressor whose activity level becomes more frenetic as the stress level increases, the negatively stressing dog will quickly "shut down," attempting to cope with a stress-inducing situation by closing it out or avoiding it. Shutting down basically comprises any form of uncharacteristic inactivity, including curling up in a ball, sleeping, turning his back, or going off to hide somewhere he may perceive as safe or quiet.

What types of situations are likely to induce stress? Depending upon the individual dog, many things can act as triggers. There are, however, a few general areas that seem to have a marked impact on nearly every dog:

Isolation

Siberians are extremely social, gregarious animals who require the company of either other dogs, other animals, or people. A dog left alone for extended periods of time is highly likely to experience stress.

Confinement

Much of the frustration resulting from confinement is caused by either visual or aural stimulation. A Siberian Husky in a fenced yard may be perfectly calm until another dog begins barking a few houses away, or until a child, a cat, or another dog runs by. It doesn't take much to set off a confined, frustrated dog.

Lack of Exercise

Daily exercise is an absolute requirement for a dog to remain physically and mentally healthy. Siberians must have an outlet for energy. Energy not expended on normal exercise will most likely be redirected as stress-related behavior of some sort.

Lack of Routine

A dog that never knows when he's going to eat, go out, or spend time with his owner will be kept in a constant state of anticipation.

Poor Health

Chronic health problems, such as hip dysplasia, arthritis, or digestive difficulties, lead to stress due to pain or discomfort. A poorly groomed dog can also suffer discomfort stress from fleas, rashes, mats in his coat, or ear infections. Siberians are very stoic by nature, and some of these problems are not always evident to us.

Mental Confusion

"Gray areas" in both training and your own general behavior can create confusion in your dog's mind. Siberians are also extremely sensitive to the emotional state of their pack, and quite capable of sensing your own feelings of anger, frustration, or anxiety. Loud, emotional outbursts can have an immediate effect on your dog, even when they are not directed at him.

Improper Diet

Food that doesn't meet your dog's nutritional needs, is lacking in essential nutrients, is unbalanced, or causes allergic reactions has a profound impact on his physical well-being, and therefore his mental and emotional state, as well.

The key to controlling the amount of stress your dog must cope with is primarily a matter of controlling your dog's environment. While we are powerless to eliminate stress entirely, we are certainly able to substantially alleviate it. It is also important to remember that only your dog decides what is or is not stressful to him—it's *his* perception that matters. Once we have learned to identify these signs of stress, we can do our best to help control it. Being a responsible owner includes being aware of our Siberians as thinking, feeling beings.

CHAPTER 6

Keeping Your Siberian Husky Happy and Healthy

BY JEAN FOURNIER

The Siberian Husky is considered by many dog experts and veterinary specialists to be one of the healthiest and most structurally sound of all dog breeds. Perhaps this can be attributed to the breed's relative genetic purity; perhaps it's just good luck. But there are some conditions every prospective owner or would-be breeder should keep in mind in order to have the healthiest and happiest Siberian possible.

BREED SPECIFIC CONDITIONS—"RED ALERT"

Cataracts and Other Eye Abnormalities

Cataracts are probably the number one hereditary problem among Siberians. A cataract is any abnormal opacity (cloudiness) of the lens or its outer covering. The opacity may range from a tiny spot (common in Siberians) to total loss of transparency. Causes of cataracts include hereditary predisposition, metabolic defects, injuries, and aging. The rate of cataract development varies from a few days to years. Any Siberian considered a breeding prospect should be examined by a board-certified ophthalmologist at least once a year, and probably more often during the first year. Eye clinics are periodically sponsored by many dog organizations, or dogs may be taken directly to various veterinary teaching hospitals where such ophthalmologists are on staff. No cataract-affected animal should ever be bred, and that goes for the other, less frequently encountered eye abnormalities found in the breed—progressive retinal atrophy (PRA), glaucoma, and corneal dystrophy.

Epilepsy

Epilepsy is relatively common in dogs and is often hereditary. Nerve cells in the brain function by the transmission of electrical impulses, but when there is excessive discharge of electrical energy in groups of brain cells, it causes a seizure or convulsion. Why this spontaneous discharge occurs is not fully understood, but in most cases the condition is hereditary in dogs. Epilepsy usually becomes apparent between 6 months and 5 years of age, and nearly all pure breeds and mixed breeds are affected. Treatment for epilepsy does not cure the disease but alleviates the condition by decreasing the frequency, duration, and severity of seizures. To learn the characteristics of seizures, consult your veterinarian.

Hypothyroidism

Hypothyroidism is a relatively common canine disorder in which the thyroid gland secretes insufficient thyroid hormones. Fortunately, it isn't life-threatening, but it does diminish the quality of life. Once diagnosed, however, this disorder is relatively easy to treat. Symptoms include weight gain, lethargy, hair loss, and aggression that may develop so gradually as to go undiagnosed. A simple blood test, however, is all that is required to identify the disease.

Zinc-Responsive Dermatosis

Zinc is an important cofactor of many critical biological functions and was originally thought to play a major role in several known skin conditions of all dogs. However, recent studies indicate that zinc deficiency is rare in most dogs. The deficiency is caused by the inability to absorb zinc in the diet and is primarily found in Siberian Huskies and Alaskan Malamutes. Skin lesions in these breeds develop despite well-balanced diets containing sufficient zinc. Affected dogs show symptoms beginning in early adulthood (at 1 to 3 years of age) and develop crusting and scaling around the mouth, chin, eyes, ears, scrotum, vulva, elbows, and other pressure points. There may also be a decreased sense of smell and taste. Signs may be intensified by physical or mental stress, including "the onset of seasons," or recent administration of anesthesia. Dogs being boarded or having faced a traumatic experience occasionally exhibit zinc deficiency syndromes. Oral zinc supplementation with increased doses for a few weeks will restore the zinc supply, which can then be maintained at fairly low doses for the dog's lifetime. It is suggested that dogs which exhibit signs of zinc deficiency not be used for breeding. It may be necessary to alert your veterinarian about possible zinc deficiency in your dog, as this syndrome was only recognized by the University of Pennsylvania Veterinary Research Department a few years ago.

Born of snow, the Siberian remains forever in love with and defined by the essence of the north. (Gene Merritt)

PREVENTIVE CARE

Immunizations

Ask your veterinarian to provide a complete immunization program for your dog. Always obtain a history of all vaccinations given when purchasing a new puppy or adult of any age. There are NO permanent shots! The following major infectious diseases contracted by dogs should be discussed with your veterinarian:

- Bordatella
- Canine distemper
- Coronavirus
- Infectious canine hepatitis
- Infectious canine respiratory diseases
- Leptospirosis
- Rabies
- Parainfluenza
- Parvovirus
- Tracheobronchitis (kennel cough)

Internal Parasites

There are several species of infectious worms that dogs may contract; however, the most common are found in practically all dogs at one time or another. These are easily diagnosed by identification during microscopic examination of the stool. Your veterinarian will discuss this important subject along with proper treatment during your dog's first visit. Do not take shortcuts in eliminating the parasites as your dog's health can be seriously jeopardized by the following parasites:

- Heartworm
- Hookworm

- Roundworms

- Tapeworms (diagnosed by stool exam or attached to hair around the anus)

- Whipworms

With heartworm, a carrier mosquito bites a dog and deposits microfilariae that travel through the dog's bloodstream, lodging in the heart to reproduce. The carrier dog is later bitten by an uninfected mosquito, which becomes infected, and then bites and infects a new host, thereby extending the contagion. The disease has been found in every state in the United States and in many foreign countries. Fortunately, preventive medication is both available and effective in both daily and monthly regimens.

External Parasites

Ticks

Tiny relatives of spiders, ticks feed exclusively on the blood of their hosts and can make the life of any infested dog very miserable indeed. There are several species of ticks and some can carry very serious diseases. Only the female tick feeds, and after she has become engorged with blood, she drops off her host to lay a huge number of eggs. These hatch in turn and the life cycle repeats itself. Ticks are easily contracted by dogs that move about in contaminated areas, especially in high grass or heavy underbrush. They will remain in one spot on the dog and are often found between the toes, behind the ears, and near the anus. A wide

variety of very effective products for ridding your dog of ticks is currently available. Consult your veterinarian for a program of eradication and control. To combat ticks you must remove them from your dog and your home environment.

Lyme Disease

This infectious disease is most commonly spread by the deer tick, which can be found in grassy areas (including your lawn) and in brushy and wooded areas. It is transmitted through the bite of the tick. Not only does Lyme disease affect dogs, but domesticated and wild animals, as well as people, can contract the disease. While not all ticks carry Lyme disease, dog owners should be vigilant during warm seasons, inspecting their Siberians every day. If caught early, Lyme disease can be treated effectively with antibiotics. There is now a 95 percent effective vaccine available from your veterinarian, who can explain the symptoms and treatment.

Flea Infestations

Fleas are small, wingless insects with flattened bodies that infest the haircoats of animals and feed on their blood. They can spread a common tapeworm of dogs, cause anemia in very severe infestations, and may carry several viral and bacterial diseases. More commonly, they may cause skin allergies resulting in rashes, sores, and a very uncomfortable dog. They are especially hard to treat in heavily coated dogs like your Siberian Husky. They like warm, damp environments, and must be treated on a systemic basis. The common mistake most

The foxy sweetness of the Siberian's gaze makes an ironic, but certainly appropriate, contrast with the mysterious black halo in this portrait. (Gene Merritt)

owners make is treating the fleas on the dog, but not the home, kennel, dog house, bed, and yard. These areas are constant sources of infestation. The best retaliation against fleas is a total flea control product for your dog and a premise-control program. Again, there are many excellent, year-round treatments that really work. It may seem costly and require an intense effort for several weeks, but it is worth every moment when you consider the comfort of your dog(s). Again, your veterinarian can walk you through the entire process from beginning to end. Remember, there are no shortcuts.

Lice

Lice are small, wingless insects that occasionally infest domestic animals. The Siberian's dense coat makes it difficult to rid your dog of lice, but it can be done with a lot of determination and effort on your part. The two types of pests are the biting louse and the sucking louse. Biting lice are extremely irritating to dogs. They do not penetrate the skin but feed on dead skin cells, body secretions, and hair. Sucking lice penetrate the skin and feed continually on the dog's blood, causing great discomfort and anemia. They are very host-specific, so dog lice do not infest people. Treatment will be tailored to your individual dog's needs, and in Siberian Huskies this typically means extreme measures for eradication. Clipping the coat often facilitates removal of the eggs, or nits, and makes treatment with insecticides easier. All dogs living with an infested dog should also be treated, along with the housing area, yard, and kennel.

Sarcoptic Mange

Sarcoptic mange is a skin disease caused by a parasitic mite, and is commonly found in wild animals, such as foxes, wolves, rabbits, and raccoons. It is highly contagious and produces intense itching, thinning of hair, and development of crusts and scabs. The mites may also infect people in close contact with an infested dog. Anyone in contact with an infected dog that develops skin lesions should consult a physician. Treatment for your dog has become quite simple, and entails one or two timely injections. Thorough cleansing and insecticidal sprays must be used on all equipment that comes in contact with the dog. Do your utmost to keep your dog(s) out of suspect outdoor areas, such as woodlands and uncultivated fields.

A moment's break from wrestling. (Cheryl Scheall)

OTHER AREAS OF CONCERN

To keep your Siberian in prime condition, feed a high quality, high protein food as described in Chapter 5, "Living with a Siberian Husky," and consult your veterinarian about any questionable symptom or irregularity, no matter how trivial it may seem. All dogs are susceptible to the following ailments and diseases, and early detection usually allows for the most effective treatment.

- Bladder stones
- Cancer
- Digestive system disease
- Heart disease
- Kidney disease
- Lick granulomas
- Liver disease
- Obesity (see Chapter 13, "Our Gentle Geriatrics")
- Tooth decay (see Chapter 7, "Grooming the Siberian Husky")

CHAPTER 7

Grooming the Siberian Husky

BY SARAH E. GAUNT

Compared to other breeds, maintaining a well-groomed Siberian is relatively simple. Not only is the Siberian Husky typically odor-free, the coat is naturally clean under most conditions. The coat is a "double coat," composed of soft undercoat and an outer coat known as the "guard hairs." The outer coat provides weather resistance while the undercoat creates warmth and protects the dog from dampness. This double coat can withstand mud, rain, and snow, and is remarkably self-cleaning. Under normal circumstances, therefore, a pet Siberian needs little more than a weekly brushing and a yearly or twice-yearly bath, but more extensive grooming during shedding periods or if the dog is being shown will help keep the animal in prime condition. Siberians also generally enjoy the individual attention of the grooming routine. The necessary tools include a metal comb, pin brush, slicker brush, coat rake, nail clipper, toothbrush, tooth scaler, and small scissors for trimming hair between toes, if necessary.

While regular brushing helps control intermittent shedding, profuse shedding occurs in Siberians twice a year. Siberian fanciers refer to this episode of hair loss as "blowing the coat." Indeed, fine tufts of

83

hair appear all over the body. (Without a powerful vacuum cleaner, these little tufts can also be found all over the house.) Once full shedding begins, frequent warm baths assist in accelerating removal of the outer coat.

Prior to bathing, use a coat rake throughout the body to remove the shedding undercoat. The slicker brush helps pull out the undercoat that is not in tufts. Whenever working on the coat, it should be moistened using a spray bottle containing water mixed with a small amount of conditioner to prevent new coat from breaking. A final combing and vigorous brushing prepares the coat for a warm bath. To avoid clogging the drain with the dense undercoat, place a plastic drain catch over the drain opening. Any pet shampoos are fine for bathing. The application of a creme rinse after shampooing makes the coat easier to comb through when dry.

Though apprehensive at first, most puppies adapt to bathing without a problem, particularly if the experience is made into a pleasant one. Put cotton balls in the ears to prevent water from getting down in the lower ear. Using baby shampoo on the head prevents the eyes from stinging. During the bath a puppy should always be praised for behaving. A treat isn't a bad idea to reinforce that bathing is an "alright" experience. Wash the body coat first. A hand-held shower head works well in the tub. Put a rubber mat on the bottom of the tub to give traction. Outdoors a simple garden hose is fine. Be especially careful to rinse the underbody. Leaving soap and creme rinse residue can cause itching and skin irritation. Towel dry and either allow the coat to dry naturally or use a forced-cool-air hair dryer. A thorough combing, using a "Greyhound" metal comb and pin brush will give your dog's clean coat additional plushness. When the comb will pass easily through the coat from back to front (against the grain, so to speak), the coat grooming is complete.

Every Siberian Husky will need an occasional bath. With regular grooming, however, the need for frequent bathing is greatly reduced. (Winter Churchill Photography)

Accustom your Siberian to the grooming table from puppy-hood. A table will make the dog behave better and will be easier on your back. (Winter Churchill Photography)

Training a young puppy to stand on a grooming table greatly simplifies the coat grooming procedure and other general care procedures. After bathing, it is a good idea to attend to your dog's nails, while they are soft and pliable, and to trim any long hair that has grown between the toes.

If there is a clicking noise when the dog walks on a hard surface, then the nails need to be trimmed. To avoid cutting too close and causing bleeding, use a flashlight to see where the vein ends. Most Siberians have light-colored nails so it is easy to find the end of the vein. Clip forward of the vein. If the vein is cut accidentally, it is not an emergency. Simply apply "Kwik-Stop"™ powder or similar coagulant to stop the bleeding. To avoid the possibility of cutting the quick, many groomers use a nail grinder, but animals must be made accustomed to the noise and slight heat created by this tool. Constant monitoring of nail growth and necessary trimming is important because over-grown nails can cause the feet to splay, a painful and unattractive condition in an older dog.

Weekly dental care is recommended in order to prevent the buildup of plaque and gum disease that can result in loss of teeth. Pet toothbrushes and flavored toothpaste are readily available. Plaque buildup is often found on the front canines and back molar teeth, especially if the dog is fed a relatively soft diet. A tooth scaler is required to remove plaque. Giving your dog rawhide chewing items will also help keep teeth clean.

Regular grooming enhances the Siberian's natural beauty. It also helps monitor the overall condition and alerts the owner to potential problems, such as skin irritation and external parasites. A commitment to scheduled grooming is well worth the effort and results in a healthy, happy friend who always relishes the physical attention and togetherness afforded by grooming sessions.

NOTE: Grooming for the show ring is more frequent and occasionally more complex. Talk to your Siberian's breeder for recommendations for enhancing your individual dog's coat quality and general appearance. It should be remembered, however, that the Siberian is, historically, one of

Keeping a Siberian's teeth clean is more than a matter of grooming. It will enhance and protect the dog's health all its life. (Winter Churchill Photography)

the so-called "natural" breeds, and overgrooming, especially with the use of mousses, sprays, and similar products, though certainly common in the show ring, is a crime against that concept.

Showing the Siberian Husky

Conformation shows sanctioned by the American Kennel Club (AKC) are competitions in which dogs are judged according to their "conformation" to a written "Breed Standard." As you might expect, dog shows are highly complex human events that combine beauty pageant with serious animal husbandry in ways that may often seem bizarre to the outside observer. On the one hand, there is all the primping and preening, hairspray and blow dryers, haste, and anxiety: All that puff, fluff, and paranoia that would appear to result from the very shallowest of human impulses. On the other hand, there is the sense that something deeper may be going on that is actually good for dogs, though there is always a degree of ambiguity on that point that must be argued out within the context of a given breed fancy. In other words, Conformation shows can be good or bad for the overall well-being of a breed, depending on those involved in that breed: who controls its written "Breed Standard," its breeding, and its judging.

But, before getting deep into a philosophical discussion of a fun activity, an explanation of the structure of dog shows is in order for prospective participants.

There are basically two tiers of competition at all-breed shows. The first consists of those dogs that are competing for championship points, awarded in competition only against others of their own breed. For most, the goal is an AKC-championship title. A small number of dogs, almost always confirmed champions, remain in competition after meeting title requirements. These are shown for Best of Breed as the best examples of their particular breeds shown on a given day. Best of Breed competition is actually a preliminary advancing the breed winners to the next level—the Variety Groups.

A top winner of the late '70s and the first Best in Show-winning Siberian bitch, Ch. Chotovodka's Ms. Kitty Russell, bred and owned by Bob Page—one of the breed's most respected judges—and wife Dorothy. (Petrulis)

Under AKC rules, all recognized breeds are classified into seven Variety Groups (Sporting, Hound, Working, Terrier, Toy, Non-Sporting and, Herding). At this level, all Best of Breed winners in a given group are eligible to compete for one of four placements. In each of the Groups, the dog that emerges as first goes on to compete with the other Group winners for the coveted Best in Show award. The dogs that place behind #1 can be credited with points in national rankings, tallied by certain publications and parent clubs, toward a variety of cumulative awards.

This second tier of competition, from Best of Breed through Best in Show, provides dog shows with a degree of high drama: famous dogs, famous handlers, poised and esteemed judges making decisions in front of hushed, reverent crowds, applause, tears of victory are all part of the spectacle. But it doesn't really have much to do with the well-being of dogs, though it no doubt has something to do with the rise or fall of a breed in the popularity charts.

It's the first tier of competition, that within a given breed, that is most important to the future health and well-being of that breed. It is here that the focus of a particular "fancy" (the owners, breeders, and exhibitors active within the breed) makes all the difference. We in Siberians are very lucky in this respect because most Siberian Husky fanciers from the 1930s through the early 1960s actively worked their dogs in harness. Most, like Lorna Demidoff, only started showing their dogs "to have something to do with the dogs during the summer months when they weren't working." From these people came the first written Standards of the breed: the basic description of size, proportion, substance, correct movement, and "type" (those aspects of body proportions, coat, markings, skull shape and size, ears, and tail carriage, that distinguishes a breed). These people knew the Siberian as a highly versatile athlete with a wonderful variety of coat colors, markings, and even eye colors. They created a Standard for dogs judged in the ring designed to maintain the Siberian's time-honored working characteristics; even though they knew as well as anyone that as soon as you begin to breed a dog more for what she looks like than what she does, you begin to walk on thin ice.

Ch. Innisfree's Sierra Cinnar, one of the breed's most significant winners and producers, was Best in Show at the famed Westminster Kennel Club show in 1980—the only Siberian to ever achieve this coveted award. "Cinnar" is shown with his handler, co-owner and friend, Trish Kanzler.

Today, we walk that same thin ice. Many more Siberians are currently exhibited in the show ring than are run on the trail, and that puts a heavy responsibility on the breeders and exhibitors of contemporary show dogs to maintain the underlying athleticism of the breed, and not just breed "cute" animals. There is always an abundance of conformation judges willing to reward pretty faces and pretty coats. If, however, those are not astutely aware of the machinery beneath the surface, they will not do the breed any great service in their selections. The same applied to the breeders and exhibitors who ignore those essential aspects of anatomy that make a Siberian potentially functional and historically correct. There is the danger that they will put aesthetic points above working ability to the breed's damage. Again, we are fortunate to have a Breed Standard that is so well-written and so clear in its emphasis on the traditional sled dog that originally came to the North American continent. But it should always be remembered that any breed CAN be turned into dolls and hothouse flowers, what people who work their dogs occasionally refer to as "paper dogs," dogs with no purpose or value except that they are AKC-registered.

So the basis of dog judging is the written Standard of each breed. Animals may be entered in a puppy class, the Novice class, the Bred-by-Exhibitor class, the

Ch. Kontoki's Natural Sinner, owned by Tommy Oelschlager, was a winner of seventeen Specialty shows, a record in the breed. He also won nine all-breed BIS and sired fifty-nine champions.

Ch. Kontoki's One Mo' Time, owned by Nan Wisniewski, Marlene DePalma and Tommy Oelschlager, won thirty-five BIS, thirteen Specialties, and sired thirty-five champions, shown here at 10 years old. (Ashbey)

American-bred class, or the Open class. At most shows, there may be a single puppy class for dogs between 6 and 12 months old, or there may be one for junior puppies (6 to 9 months) and another for senior puppies (9 to 12 months). A 12 to 18 months class is for young dogs yet to mature fully. The Novice class is reserved for dogs or their handlers who have not yet won a blue ribbon in competition, and is seldom seen except at Specialty shows (for a single breed only). The Bred-by-Exhibitor class is reserved for those dogs bred and owned by their handlers, and is an especially prestigious class at Specialty shows. The American-bred class is open to all dogs born within the United States by reason of a mating which also took place in the United States. Usually this class will contain

less experienced or less mature dogs than those entered in the Open class, which is open to any registered animal over 6 months of age, including champions, regardless of her birthplace.

Up to four placements are awarded in each class, and then all the first-prize winners within each sex (dogs are judged first, then bitches) compete for Winners Dog or Winners Bitch awards, and these two winners are the only animals to receive championship points on that day. A Reserve Winners award is also made in each sex to the animals judged the second best in a given sex among the class animals shown that day. However,

Ch. Kontoki's E-I-E-I-O, owned by N. Wisniewski, B. Moye, M. DePalma and T. Oelschlager, holds the record as the top-winning show Siberian of all time with sixty BIS awards and sixteen Specialty Bests. (Joe C)

Ch. Kontoki's Uh-Huh!, owned by Abel and Andrea Amaral, Marlene DePalma, and Tommy Oelschlager, won nine all-breed BIS and six Specialties. (Ashbey)

no championship points are attached to these "honorable mentions" unless the Winners Dog or Winners Bitch is subsequently disqualified on some technicality—an animal improperly entered, for instance.

At this point, the Winners Dog and Winners Bitch reenter the ring, along with any champions entered for Best of Breed competition that day, and the following awards are made: Best of Breed to the animal of either sex deemed to be the best example of that breed that day; Best of Opposite Sex to Best of Breed to the best animal of the other sex; and Best of Winners is given to either Winners Dog or Winners Bitch, depending on which the judge thinks is better. Championship points are awarded on the basis of how many

animals of a given sex are shown (from one to five points), and are awarded only to the Winners Dog and Winners Bitch. The animal awarded Best of Winners, however, is eligible for the maximum number of points awarded that day, even if awarded in the other sex. In other words, a Winners Dog who was eligible to win only two points, according to the number of class males entered, may beat the Winners Bitch who took three points and thereby earn three points himself. In such instances, the defeated Winners would still keep the points he or she has already won.

Despite all the hype and hoopla attending American dog shows (they are considerably more low-key in Europe), the underlying purpose is simply the identification of the best breeding stock to be used to perpetuate a given breed, and as such, they serve an essential purpose. The system is not perfect, of course; politics and bad judging frequently predominate, and too many judges are approved to judge more breeds than anyone could possibly know well enough. But it is at dog shows that the future of most breeds is fashioned, as today's winner becomes tomorrow's puppy producer. So it is, above all else (or perhaps beneath all else), the place where the future of a breed is at stake.

ACQUIRING A SIBERIAN HUSKY SHOW PROSPECT

Anyone wanting to compete in AKC-sanctioned Conformation shows should understand that in a breed with such huge numbers of contestants as the Siberian Husky, the undertaking has the potential to be difficult, expensive, and often frustrating. But showing can also be a challenge, bursting with fun and rewards, providing you have patience and the right attitude. The right attitude amounts to a kind of humility; you realize going in that the overall good of the breed is much more important than any one individual dog or exhibitor. You remember that all dogs have faults and that different judges will view different faults from different perspectives. Finally, you should never stop learning what makes for a truly superior Siberian, in terms of specific elements of structure and type, as well as in overall balance.

You should also have a deep reserve of patience when it comes to acquiring a show

Ch. Solocha Kasan Ghost Rider, owned by Chuck and Betty Charlton, a top contender in the early '90s.

Ch. Wildestar's Fire N' Ice, owned by Brenda and Albert Valletta, winner of the 1996 National Specialty. (Kohler)

Ch. Brandon's Sundance Kid, owned by Danny and Margit Brand, a top contender in the late '90s. (Lennah)

prospect. Almost all Siberian puppies are cute, and nearly everyone owning one believes it is the most beautiful animal imaginable. But the subtleties of anatomy and type are too numerous for anyone but an expert on the breed to take into account to make a judgment about the "showability" of a given dog. So seek out those "experts." You'll find them at dog shows where, unfortunately, almost all exhibitors think of themselves in that category. It takes some time, therefore, to winnow the wheat from the chaff in terms of advice and information, but the time spent looking at animals and talking to breeders is time well spent. Be wary of forming your own aesthetic responses too quickly. Almost everyone is susceptible to falling for either the "big bears," those imposing large-boned animals, or the "teddy bears," the fluffy, short-legged cuties. Many

judges also fall for one of these two extremes because they can be so eye-catching, but they are equally wrong in terms of the Standard, and equally wrong in terms of the history and function of the breed. Look for the moderate, fluid dogs whose movement seems truly effortless, and then talk to the breeders who own or have bred these animals.

In talking to breeders about acquiring a show prospect, be upfront about exactly what you want. It is better to acquire a yearling, already show-trained, than a puppy, simply because there is less you need a crystal ball for. The dog is already close to what it is going to be, even though it may seem a bit gawky. Such an animal is often hard to find, however, since few breeders are willing to part with a truly promising yearling. Many breeders may be willing to sell a slightly less impressive dog of the same age, and that yearling might be entirely satisfactory for your first show dog. No breeder parts with his or her very best, unless by accident or in extreme circumstances; and that's simply the law of self-preservation among breeders. Put yourself in the breeder's place. Where does the next generation come from if you routinely part with your best? And how long can you hope to stay competitive if you're only breeding your second best?

Once you've read and studied the Standard deeply enough to understand it, attended a few dog shows, and met a breeder, or even several breeders, you like and trust, you're ready to acquire a show prospect. Be prepared to wait, if necessary, and trust the breeder's advice. No one has a crystal ball, so if you do acquire a puppy (as most people do), no one can predict infallibly what that puppy will grow up to be. But breeders with experience and a proven track record do know their lines and can make quite educated guesses about the potential of a given puppy. So, if possible, give the breeder you go with the leeway to help you: Don't insist on the blackest or the biggest or whatever in a litter. Believe in the potential of the puppy the breeder helps you choose. One of the great advantages of working with a breeder living fairly close to you is that you get to see the puppies and usually the parents, and you can have that breeder as a mentor. Excellent animals can be acquired from long distance, of course, but it makes the learning process more difficult.

Bait helps the show training process, even when the puppy is off lead. (JoLynn Stresing)

LEARNING TO SHOW

The breeder will help you develop your new Siberian Husky puppy into a show dog by suggesting local handling classes or puppy kindergartens, as well as informing you about upcoming match shows (which are more or less practice events where no championship points are awarded and the main interest is in having fun with your dog without much pressure). Socializing an animal for the show ring is a somewhat delicate matter, since it only takes one bad experience for a puppy to decide she doesn't like it. Getting caught next to a roaring generator, or being attacked by a big, hairy dog whose owner is asleep at the switch and not controlling his or her animal—these are the kinds of events you do not want to introduce into your animal's early vision of dog shows.

Remember that you're making a long-term investment in the socialization of this dog, so don't push too hard. It is far easier in the long run to bring a rowdy, rambunctious puppy under control than it is to bring a highly submissive, overly compliant Siberian back up to the level of a flashy show dog. So keep training sessions short and FUN. Even in her early show experiences, it is far better to let your dog make a fool of you, as long as she's having fun, than to expect a highly regimented performance. Too many puppies are asked by their owners to perform impeccably at an age when they should not have to be so polished. The frequent result is that, as the animal reaches a level of maturity where she could seriously compete for major awards, she is so bored by the process that her performance is totally lackluster. So keep it light, keep it fun, and be sure to have fun yourself.

RINGSIDE DISCRETION

You will quickly discover that the ringside is a curious culture—a Tower of Babel, or *babble,* in which everyone has something to say, and almost no one is interested in what anyone else has to say. Some few may actually have something nice to say about your dog, most will have nothing to say, and some will even feel compelled to tell you everything wrong with your dog. Smile back sweetly, listen to what everyone has to say, say as little as possible, and then, at some later time, discuss some of the issues with your mentor.

Eventually, you will develop a perspective and come to understand where various factions stand in terms of their viewpoint on the breed. It is a somewhat painful process of initiation since most newcomers are so excited about their new dog that they naturally suppose everyone else will feel the same. Unfortunately, you are too often perceived as just another competitor in a very tough game, and you will come to see that the middle syllables of "competition" are pronounced "petty." You will also discover, if you are not careful, the inevitable law of ringside commentary—that as soon as you notice something really bad about a dog and mention it out loud, you will find the owner of that dog standing right next to you!

So it really pays to bite your tongue.

But there are also some wonderful people you will meet at ringside, people who have devoted decades to the breed they love, and who are always free and open with new people. Often they are among the most senior of the Siberian Husky breeders, with little or nothing to prove, and so are more approachable. (Just don't try to buttonhole them when they are hurriedly grooming a dog, or are standing at ringside with a dog to be shown in the next class.) You will also meet people who are themselves just starting out, with whom you will have much in common, and with whom you may find yourself staying up half the night "talking dogs." And, with a little luck and a lot of focus and fortitude, you may find yourselves the prominent breeders of the next decade, helping the newcomers of tomorrow.

Above all, it is important to enter this sport slowly and judiciously. Too many new enthusiasts want to jump in with both feet, acquiring umpteen different "promising" puppies from umpteen different breeders, certain that at least one of these will turn into the "great" show dog that will win them lots of blue ribbons and "put them on the map." In the first place, each truly promising animal deserves much more individual time and attention than this process would allow. In the second, each animal will teach you important things about the breed: the variety of personality, for instance, and all sorts of things about anatomy. You'll learn about faults, especially if you're handling yourself. You'll learn about real virtues of type and structure, if you're paying close attention. And you'll learn to see the competition much more clearly. So even if your first Siberian has a noticeable fault or two, stick with it for a while simply as a learning experience. You may find the fault does not, in the long run, present such a great problem (most every dog has at least three things that could be improved). And the

Ch. Wildestar's Cat Ballou (Ch. Wildestar's Fire N' Ice ex Ch. Demavand's Sappho) is shown here winning the 1998 National Specialty under judge H. M. Cresap over a total entry of 1,343 Siberians, including 11 champions. Owned by Albert and Brenda Valletta (handling), she was bred by Brenda Valletta and Michael Jenning.

truth is, we all make mistakes in developing our first show dogs, and it really is better to make almost all your mistakes with one dog, rather than spreading them over five or six. So if you devote yourself to this first animal for at least eighteen months or two years, and she doesn't turn out to be truly competitive, you haven't wasted two years, you've gained them—in experience and perspective—and you're ready to make a far more judicious second choice.

In all this, I've presupposed the "owner handler" approach to showing, but, of course, the Siberian ring is highly competitive these days, and there are lots of professional handlers in the ring. Nevertheless, I believe there is no better way to get to know a breed than to handle your dog yourself. If, after going through the basic training with the dog, you decide that it is a better strategy to hire a handler, it is certainly an option, but not one that will teach you as much as quickly.

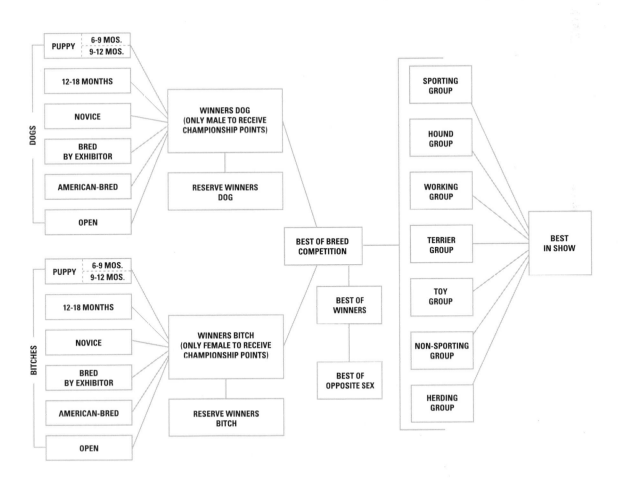

CHAPTER 9

Obedience, Agility, and Other Fun and Useful Things

BY LOIS LEONARD, OBEDIENCE CHAIR, SIBERIAN HUSKY CLUB OF AMERICA

OBEDIENCE

Obedience can be defined as the training that turns an unruly, out of control animal into a much-loved member of the family. Classes are held in park districts, private obedience clubs, schools, and even local animal shelters. In these classes, handlers learn what the basics consist of and how to teach them to their canine companions: to sit, lie down, stay in a specific spot, and come on command.

Siberian Huskies are not always the easiest dogs to train because of many factors, not the least of which are their intelligence and independent nature. Obedience training is repetitive, and a Siberian will only take so much repetition before he thinks, "Okay, we've done that, now what?" Also, Siberians are possessed of a wonderful sense of humor; when they make a mistake, and people laugh, they want to repeat the error which brought them the attention. In obedience school, they are often described as the class clowns.

But Siberian Huskies can be trained and can perform very well indeed. The same qualities that make it more challenging to train a Siberian Husky have propelled many to excellence in the competitive sport of Obedience Trials, and found them earning titles ranging from the basic CD (Companion Dog) all the way through and including the OTCH (Obedience Trial Champion).

Competitive Obedience is a sport that may be enjoyed by anyone with a purebred dog. The American Kennel Club (AKC) licenses clubs all over the United States to hold Obedience Trials year-round, both indoors and outdoors. At indoor trials, rubber nonslip mats are used. Similar competitions are available through the United Kennel Club (UKC), and in Canada through the Canadian Kennel Club (CKC); many other countries also support this type of organization. Obedience is unlike many other competitions; earning a title is based solely on receiving a qualifying score and bears no relationship to the scores of any other entry in the class.

No matter what level, the basic requirements include a series of exercises for which the dog has

"The Siberian Husky is not a disobedient dog, rather a dog intelligent enough to see all the available options and independent enough to act upon them."—Pat Tetrault (© 1996 Bohm Mariazzo Photography)

been schooled and then performs according to what is described as the theoretically perfect performance. When dog and handler enter the ring, the judge "gives" them 200 points. Then, for each error, a deduction is made. Each exercise is assigned a specific point total, and the team must earn more than 50 percent of the available points. The total number of points must exceed 170 for a dog to earn a "leg." Three "legs," under three different judges, are required for a title to be awarded.

The three AKC Obedience levels are: Novice, in which beginning dogs try for the title Companion Dog (CD); Open, in which more advanced dogs try for the Companion Dog Excellent title (CDX); and finally Utility, which is still more demanding, and dogs can earn the Utility Dog degree (UD). Advanced titles for which a dog must have earned its Utility degree are Utility Dog Excellent (UDX) and Obedience Trial Champion (OTCH).

In the Novice class, dog and handler must perform six exercises: heel on lead with a figure eight, stand for examination, heel off lead, recall, one-minute sit, and three-minute down. The first four exercises are judged one dog at a time, while the last two are judged with all dogs entered in the class performing in a group, with twelve dogs tested at a time, lined up approximately three feet apart. On command of the judge, handlers tell their dogs to "stay," leave as a group and walk to the opposite side of the ring, then turn and face the dogs. The dogs may not move from their specified positions, get up, whine, sniff, or otherwise make errors. When the allotted time has expired, the judge issues the instruction, "Return to your dogs." The exercise is not complete until the judge states, "Exercise finished."

Rashaun's Niki Tiki Tavi, CD, a lovely piebald bitch, takes to the air.

The exercises become more difficult in Open. Dogs heel only off lead. The other exercises are drop on recall, retrieve on the flat, retrieve over the high jump, and the broad jump. Retrieving is done with a wooden or molded plastic dumbbell of a size commensurate with the size of the dog. Sits and downs are group exercises, but they are performed with handlers out of sight outside the ring and require a three-minute sit and a five-minute down.

Utility is the most complex and requires the dog to work the majority of time away from the handler. The signal exercise is heeling without any verbal commands, followed by a series of hand signals issued to the dog from a distance. The dog is left in a standing position; handler proceeds to the end of the ring, then turns to face the dog. Upon instructions from the judge, handler gives hand signals for the dog to down, then sit, come to a front position, and return to heel. Next are the scent discrimination exercises: eight small dumbbells, four leather and four metal, are placed twenty feet from the dog. A fifth article, one of each type, is scented by the handler by rubbing hands on all surfaces of the article, and placed in the pile by the judge. The dog must find it, pick it up, return to the handler, and give it when commanded. In the glove exercise, three white work-style gloves are laid on the mat or grass halfway across the ring, one each at left, center, and right. The judge gives the command to retrieve glove #1, #2, or #3, the handler and dog turn to face the proper glove, and the handler signals the dog to retrieve it. The dog must go directly to the proper glove, pick it up, return, and give it to the handler upon command. The moving stand requires the dog to stop in the middle of a heeling exercise when signaled, and stand without moving as the handler continues an additional ten feet away, turns, and faces the dog. The judge physically goes over the dog from head to tail and then tells the handler to finish, at which point the handler commands the dog to come to heel position.

Last, but by no means least, is directed jumping. A high or solid jump and a bar jump, at a height determined by the height of the dog, are located to the left and right of center. The handler sends the dog to the opposite end of the ring and commands the dog to sit. Then, with a hand/arm and a verbal signal, the handler directs the dog to

OTCH LoJan's Very Special Sula, Can. CDX, Sch., AD, owned and shown by Lois Leonard, is only the second Siberian and first bitch of the breed to earn the OTCH degree and one of the top Siberian Obedience performers of all time. Her impressive record includes two National Specialty and eighteen area Specialty High in Trial awards and 246 AKC qualifying scores. Here she goes through her well-schooled paces in a scent discrimination exercise.

jump the obstacle the judge has indicated, and repeats this for the second jump.

Dogs may earn a UDX once they have a Utility title by competing in both the Open and Utility classes at the same show. These dogs must earn qualifying scores of 170 or better in both classes at ten different shows to earn the title. Requirements for an OTCH are more difficult. Utility dogs compete for placements in Open and Utility. To earn points, they must place either first or second, with points determined by the number of dogs defeated in each class. Three first places are required, at least one each in Open and Utility, and a total of 100 points must be accumulated. A dog seeking the points is also competing against the many dogs that have already earned their OTCH titles.

Competitive Obedience has, in recent years, become increasingly more precise. Judges carry a mental picture of that theoretically perfect performance in each exercise and score each dog against this standard, which combines the utmost in willingness, enjoyment, and precision on the part of the dog with naturalness, gentleness, and smoothness of the handler.

At this writing, only two Siberian Huskies have earned Obedience Trial Championships. Two others have been awarded UDX titles, although there are several "knocking at the door." As Obedience enthusiasts learn that properly trained Siberian Huskies can and will perform exceptionally well, more and more are earning advanced titles — and with high scores!

AGILITY

Agility, developed in England in the late 1970s, is a dog sport that has become increasingly popular all across the United States. Although there are strict rules and regulations as in any competition, it does not require the precision of Obedience, it is extremely exciting to both perform and watch, and dogs, especially Siberian Huskies, love it.

Basic obedience is a necessity for anyone wishing to participate in Agility, because all activities

Ch. KeeNonNe's Wolfpak Leader, UDX, OA, one of only three Siberians to receive a UDX title. (Lorraine Paglini)

AKC and WWKC Ch. UCDX Olympus Seminole Wind, UDX, CGC, one of only three Siberians to achieve a UDX title. (Susan Norton)

are off lead. Precise heeling, as in Obedience, is not necessary, but quick responses to sit, down, here, go out, or similar commands are of the utmost importance. Not only is the dog judged on accuracy in performing over the obstacles, but time is a factor as well. Dogs may wear buckle collars, but no hanging tags or attachments are allowed, nor are choke, pinch, prong, electric, or dummy electric collars. Food or toys are also prohibited in competition but are used extensively in training the dog.

Three different organizations present Agility Trials; each has its own regulations, and there are many differences in the requirements for type of obstacles and course layout, as well as the relationship between height of dog and jump. At the same time, they possess many similarities. Obstacles are usually colorful to the eye and distinctive in shape while remaining functional. These include simple bar and panel jumps, as well as more complex double and triple jumps such as seen in equine competitions, and unique types such as a tire and a window jump. Other obstacles are a dog walk, see-saw, A-frame, pause table, open tunnel (similar to a child's vinyl crawl tunnel), closed tunnel (having a 24" x 24" framed opening with a fabric chute 12 to 15 feet long), sway bridge, and weave poles.

An Agility course is designed by the judge. Each course has certain required obstacles and there is a minimum number of these, determined by the degree or level of competition, and the judge may include optional obstacles. Classes are

Take that, Air Jordan: Sierra Krasvivaya Natasha, CDX.

divided based solely on the height of the dog at the withers, and not by breed. The different organizations determine their own divisions; in AKC Agility, there are five: 8, 12, 16, 20, and 24 inches. As in Obedience there are degrees of difficulty: AKC levels are Novice, Open, Excellent, and Master Excellent; a dog must earn qualifying scores at three different trials under two different judges to earn each title. Similar to Obedience, a dog may earn a title no matter what the individual score is in relation to others entered in the class.

TRACKING

Tracking for Siberian Huskies is simply "doin' what comes naturally," since they LOVE tracking wildlife. The difficulty occurs when the handler has to convince a Siberian to follow an old, boring, stinky human shoe track and make the dog believe human scent is more fun than chasing *critters*. The AKC offers two Tracking titles; the CKC has similar degrees offered, but major differences exist in the requirements. Titles may be earned without comparison to scoring of any other dogs in the trial. In AKC Tracking, the first title is the Tracking Dog degree (TD); this requires a dog to follow a track between 440 and 500 yards long, aged between a half hour and two hours, complete designated turns (up to five), and indicate the article dropped at the end of the track. The dog does not have to pick up the article, usually a brown glove, just indicate it to the handler who picks it up. "Aging" refers to the length of time between the laying of the track and its actual use, while "leg" refers to the straight parts of the track between the turns.

After the dog has been awarded a TD, the team may enter Tracking Dog Excellent (TDX) trials, which are more difficult. To earn this title, the dog must follow a track between 800 and 1,000 yards long, with five or more turns, four articles, and having two cross tracks. This track is aged between three to five hours.

FLYBALL

Flyball is a fast-paced, exciting sport, and as much fun for the spectators as it is for the participants. It

Defying gravity: U-CDX Ch. Sierra Sch. Roo Suba, UD, CGC, owned by Jacqueline Root, skillfully negotiates the Agility A-frame.

Many top Obedience Trial contenders are also competitive show or running dogs. This one displays beautiful type.

is a relay race, with two teams consisting of four dogs each, one dog from each team running simultaneously. Upon the sound of the judge's whistle, a dog from each team is released by his/her handler, jumps four hurdles, and steps on a pedal on the flyball box, which tosses a tennis ball into the air. The dog must catch the ball, turn around, jump the four hurdles again, and bring the ball back across the start/finish line, where the next dog eagerly awaits his or her turn.

There are three divisions: Novice, Open, and Championship. The only difference in the divisions is the racing time for the four dogs, with Novice over 28 seconds, Open over 24 but less than 28 seconds, and Championship under 24 seconds. Titles earned are: Flyball Dog, Flyball Dog Excellent, and Flyball Dog Champion.

Most Flyball Dogs have also earned Obedience titles and compete in Agility. The fast pace of flyball helps in both the conformation and Obedience rings by keeping the dogs in top condition, alert, and responsive to commands.

CANINE GOOD CITIZEN

The American Kennel Club has endorsed the Canine Good Citizenship (CGC) program as a means to promote responsible pet ownership. It is open to both purebred and mixed breed dogs, with CGC tests given under approved guidelines and certificates presented upon successful completion of the test.

There are ten separate tests in the CGC program. Guidelines are very open, allowing evaluators to make decisions based on what makes a

Backpacking is an increasingly popular sport among Siberian fanciers, and Obedience training makes it possible. The dogs are Kaberu's Fenris Red Wolf, CDX (left) and Gitana's Flying Loki. They are owned by Beatrice Infante and Sheldon Finkelstein.

Now this is SERIOUS backpacking with a serious pack leader.

Dick and Linda Stehlik's Siberians on the Salmon River have been given a "down-stay" command.

3. Walk on a Loose Lead, Out for a Walk—Upon instruction from evaluator, dog and handler execute right, left, and about turns.

4. Walk Through a Crowd—Handler and dog walk through several evaluators milling around.

5. Sit for Exam—With dog in sitting position, evaluator pets dog.

6. Sit and Down on Command—Dog executes each position on command of handler.

7. Stay in Position (sit or down)—Handler chooses position, gives command to stay, walks away from dog to a distance of 20 feet, and returns. Dog must stay in place until handler returns to heel position.

good pet, rather than adherence to a standard of perfection. The intent of the test is to give pet owners an easily achievable goal, since most do not either want or need to go through months of classes to enter in order to gain the control necessary to pass. A dog which earns a CGC certificate is the kind of dog you would like to own, would be safe with children, welcome as a neighbor, makes its owner happy, and isn't making someone else unhappy.

The tests include:

1. Appearance and Grooming—Evaluator brushes the dog and makes a thorough hands-on examination.

2. Accepting a Stranger—Evaluator walks up to the handler and dog, shakes hands, and carries on a brief conversation.

"Just follow the big dog"—Siberians at the Bitteroot Wilderness waiting for their directions.

A retrieve in tandem is beautifully executed by Ch. Chuchinka's Tarsiut of Avatuk, CDX (left) and Chuchinka's Kasha Star. Both dogs were bred by Bob and Loreen Bridges.

8. Reaction to Another Dog—Handler and dog heel past another handler and dog approaching from the opposite direction

9. Reaction to Distractions—Uses loud, noisy distractions provided, such as a child's wagon loaded with rattling stones.

10. Dog Left Alone—Dog is left by handler in a restrained situation for five minutes.

TEMPERAMENT TESTING

The American Temperament Test Society (ATTS) sponsors temperament tests. Any dog over 12 months of age may participate, both purebred and mixed breeds. Dogs who pass the requirements are issued a certificate and a TT number, and this title is listed behind the dog's name.

Test officials consist of the test organizer and/or chief tester, two testers licensed by the Society, a secretary, and six assistants at the "stations." All testers evaluate the dogs simultaneously. Dogs are scored on each subject from zero to ten; if any one tester fails a dog in any category, it is considered as having failed the entire temperament test. Failure may be because of shyness, hiding behind the handler or panicking, or showing aggression when not provoked. The testers do take into consideration the dog's breed, age, sex, and past training experiences.

The test begins with the dog walking on a loose lead to the first station, where it is approached by a neutral stranger, who simply shakes hands with the handler and walks away. At the second station, a friendly stranger approaches and pets the dog after greeting the handler. Next is the hidden noise test. The tester is hidden from view and rattles a can or bucketful of rocks, coins, screws, etc.; the dog is expected to investigate the noise. The handler may encourage the dog but must concentrate on the object and may not force the dog in any manner.

At the next station, the dog's back is turned, and the tester fires two gunshots. The team then proceeds toward a tester who is seated with an umbrella in hand. Several feet before they reach him, he pops the umbrella open. The dog is expected to investigate by touching or sniffing the umbrella; encouragement must be limited.

While heading toward the next station, handler and dog will walk over some plastic material and some grating. Upon reaching the final station, a stranger appears, waving a stick and acting in a threatening manner. When he disappears, the test is complete.

Judges inform the handler promptly whether the team has qualified. The score is averaged out, and the results provided when the certificate arrives.

BACKPACKING

The Siberian Husky's history is all about getting something from point A to point B. It is no surprise, therefore, that the Siberian is now lending himself to the sport of backpacking.

Siberian enthusiasts are finding, to their delight that the breed not only makes great company on the trail, but that he is an asset on some of the most rugged hikes possible.

If you would like to go backpacking with your Siberian you can find the names and addresses of outfitters specializing in the equipment you will need to hit the trail with your Siberian. Common sense should fuel your movements in backpacking as it should with all your outdoor activity.

(Cheryl Scheall)

CHAPTER 10

Training For the Trail

BY JANE STEFFEN

THE EQUIPMENT

To a beginner, the array of dog sledding equipment can be overwhelming, and purchasing only the basics means a considerable investment in the sport. Costly mistakes can be avoided by reading books and studying catalogs to learn the purpose for each piece of equipment, where the very best quality is necessary and where a less expensive piece will perform equally well. Most equipment is purchased from well-established mail-order outfitters operated by dog sledders who can provide product information and advice on equipment selection.

A wheeled rig replaces the dog sled in warm regions or those with minimal snowfall; in the Snow Belt, rigs are used for early training. Available in several sizes and designs, rigs have three or four wheels, a steering mechanism, and brakes. The smaller, lighter models work best with a team of four or fewer dogs; heavy-duty models provide the control needed for a larger team.

Sleds

Although a few high-tech models have been recently introduced, most dog sleds are made from hardwood, usually birch or white ash, and must be extremely strong, flexible, and lightweight. There are three basic sled types—sprint, toboggan, and freight. Sprint sleds, the smallest and lightest, are excellent for recreational use and short races. For longer races, where equipment and supplies must be carried, the toboggan, with its longer bed and lower center of gravity, is the sled of choice. Originally used to haul supplies, the freight sled is the largest and heaviest of the three types. Today, it is often used for dog sled trips in resort areas.

The parts of a sled are fastened together either with bolts or hand-tied with rawhide or nylon cord. Bolted sleds, the least expensive, are an excellent choice for a beginner. Hand-tied or lashed sleds are more flexible, durable, and easier to repair, especially on the trail. The building of dog sleds has long been revered as a craft and the builders as artisans. Sleds designed and built by New Hampshire's legendary Ed Moody are still in demand after his passing and are the prized possession of many a dog sledder.

The Gang Line

The gang line is a heavy-duty polyethylene or cable line that runs between the dogs to the sled. Each dog, except the leader, is hitched to the gang line by a neckline at the collar and a tug line at the back of the harness. A single leader is hitched at the harness to the lead section of the gang line; dual-leaders may also be coupled at the collars by a short neckline. Here, the importance of high-quality hardware cannot be overemphasized. Brass snaps for the neck and tug lines and a high-test, locking, aluminum carabiner for attaching the gang line to the sled bridle are strongly recommended.

Hitching dogs in pairs is preferred and many dog sledders use a modular gang line that consists of sections, each with neck and tug lines for a pair of dogs. The sections are looped together and repairs can be easily made by removing and replacing any damaged section. This system also allows the gang line to be shortened or lengthened, depending on the number of dogs being run. For additional security, an extra line, 12 to 14 inches long, comes off the main gang line and attaches to the sled or rig, serving as a backup should the main line fail. To help absorb the shocks created by the team starting and stopping, a bungee is inserted between the gang line and the sled bridle.

Collar and Harness

A limited-slip collar is both functional and comfortable for a working Siberian. Made from nylon webbing, it adjusts to fit a dog's neck and tightens about two inches when tension is applied, securely holding the dog without any danger of choking.

Harnesses transfer the power from the dogs to the sled and should fit comfortably without restricting movement. Designed for specific activities, harnesses come in three types—weight pulling, racing, and freighting. For recreational or competitive sledding, the Siberian uses an X- or H-back harness. A new design, the collared-neck, fits very snugly to keep any pressure off a dog's shoulder blades. Most harnesses are made from nylon webbing with fleece or pile padding around the neck and down the breastplate with a nylon loop at the back for attaching the tug line. A newer fabrication uses closed-cell foam covered with

ripstop nylon to prevent moisture from being
absorbed by the harness.

Other Essential Equipment

An essential piece of equipment, the *snow hook* is
the only safe and secure way to anchor a team
while it is stopped. Made from heavy steel, the
snow hook is carried in a holder fastened to the
sled within easy reach of the driver. One end of a
seven foot rope is attached to the snow hook; the
other end is looped and connected to the gang
line carabiner. To set the hook, the driver pushes it
into the snow as soon as the team is stopped, then
stomps it on the hook's cross bar.

The *brake pad* is a small section of snowmobile
track that can supplement or replace the sled's standard claw brake. It is attached to the back stations of
the sled and rests between the runners. Excellent for
icy conditions or rough terrain, the pad can gently
slow the team or completely stop it, depending on
the amount of pressure applied by the driver's foot.

The *snub line* is a heavy rope that secures a
team to an immovable object while the dogs are
being hitched to the gang line. One end of the
rope is attached to the gang line carabiner; the
other has a quick-release snap that allows for fast
release of the team when tension is applied.

The easiest and safest way to secure a number
of dogs before or after a run or on trail overnights
is by the use of a *picket line*. It is strung between
two immovable objects and has individual dog
drop lines with swivel snaps placed at five-foot
intervals. A cable line adds security by discouraging
dogs from chewing.

*"Over the hill and through the trees": Training for the
Iditarod. (Joe Asarisi)*

*A dog truck like this with the sled carried on top is the
vehicle of choice for serious competitive sled racers. (Joe
Asarisi)*

A *dog box* rests on a truck much like a cap to safely and comfortably transport the dogs. Each compartment holds one dog along with straw or shavings for bedding. Most designs have storage space for equipment and a flat roof for carrying the dog sled, but the design and size of a dog box are limited only by the owner's imagination. Before purchasing or building a box, talk with owners about the pros and cons of various designs.

High-fashion Iditarod wear. (Joe Asarisi)

Protective Accessories

A Siberian Husky's thick double coat serves as insulation against the elements and, unlike many mixed-breed sled dogs, a Siberian does not require the additional protection of a dog coat. Booties are used to protect feet from abrasions and cuts caused by icy conditions or rough trails. Most booties are made from fleece and secured with Velcro™ straps, but the soft material does not last very long. Competitive dog sledders have begun using booties made from more wear-resistant fabrics, such as Cordura™ and nylon-coated pack cloth.

DRESSING THE SLEDDER

Gore-Tex™ and Polartec™ have revolutionized outdoor clothing making it weather-resistant, lightweight, and comfortable. Although not inexpensive, a combination of the two is an ideal choice for dog sledding. Rubber boots are still the footwear of choice for keeping feet warm and dry. Hands are very susceptible to frostbite, so a good pair of gloves or mittens is a must. A waterproof outer mitt with a fleece liner is an excellent choice and allows the outer mitt to be removed when working with equipment or dogs. It is not necessary to spend a fortune on clothing, but whatever the choice, keeping warm and dry on the trail is important for a driver's comfort and safety.

THE DOG TEAM

Many beginners, particularly youngsters, start sledding with one or two dogs. Four-dog teams are quite popular as they can be run recreationally and, as a driver gains experience, competitively in sprint classes. In dog sledding, top performance is achieved by the quality rather than the quantity of dogs. Charles Belford, regarded as one of the most successful dog drivers in history, won fifty-seven of sixty-four races with a large team from a relatively small kennel. Belford categorized every dog that came through his kennel as A—makes the team, B—good possibility, C—time will tell, or 0—do not keep, retaining only As and Bs with an occasional promising C. A beginner should keep in mind that not only is a small team easier to train, it is also less expensive to maintain. The cost of food, veterinary care, and sledding equipment quickly escalates as the number of dogs increases. The size of a team can be gradually increased as the sledder's interest in the sport and knowledge of dog care grows.

On a team of one or two, the dogs are hitched at the harness to the lead section of a gang line; dual-leaders are run side-by-side and may also be coupled at the collars by a short neckline. With three or more, a full gang line is used and the dogs run at positions called lead, swing or point, team, and wheel.

At the head of the team is the lead dog. In this position, speed is necessary, but intelligence and trail sense are more important qualities. A leader must be self-assured, willing to take commands, and not easily frightened by unfamiliar situations. Lead dogs are classified as trail or gee/haw leaders, and while both set the team's pace and focus on the trail ahead, only a gee/haw leader responds to voice commands from the driver.

Behind the leader are the swing or point, team, and wheel dogs. Fast and strong, the swing

After the run "Belle" has had, she's entitled to pant.

dogs help turn the team, and on a small team, three or four dogs, provide the power. Since their eyes are constantly on the leader, they can, if necessary, take over. On larger teams, the swing dogs are often second-string leaders. All the dogs between the swing and wheel position are considered team dogs, the heart and engine of the team. Directly in front of the sled are the wheel dogs. Usually the strongest members of a team, they help turn the sled and must constantly pull to keep the line to the sled tight.

Experienced dog sledders recommend that dogs occasionally rotate positions. The leader will,

Teamwork is an essential ingredient of competitive sled racing. (Cheryl Scheall)

grown, they are still too immature physically and mentally for the demands of running on a team of seasoned adults. Their bones and muscles will continue to develop until about 18 months of age, and they lack the mental stamina needed to handle stress and unfamiliar situations. Expecting too much too quickly can destroy a young dog's natural desire to run and ruin any chance of it becoming a good sled dog.

Older puppies can be harnessed and taught to pull light objects, such as a small log or two by four. Paired with veterans, young adults can be run on a small team for short distances over gentle trails. Older inexperienced dogs should also be paired with veterans, and distance and speed increased as the team's level of fitness increases. Jean Bryar, an accomplished dog sledder herself, trained teams for both her husband Keith and Dick Moulton. She started all young dogs in the wheel position, gradually moving them up on the team until she found the best position for each. Only after a full season of sledding were potential leaders put up front alongside a veteran lead dog.

most likely, only want to lead and should remain at the front of the team, perhaps paired with a younger dog who exhibits lead dog potential. Should an injury occur during the season, the dogs may be required to shift positions. By experimenting, a driver will have a better sense of where to hitch the dogs.

Building a team with young or inexperienced dogs will take time and patience. Although older puppies and young adults appear to be fully

THE LANGUAGE OF DOG SLEDDING

In dog sledding, specific terminology is used by a driver to communicate with the lead dog. Trained to respond to a driver's voice commands, a good gee/haw leader is a valuable asset on any team and a necessity on a large one. To ensure uniformity throughout the sport, the following commands are used:

Gee—Turn right

Haw—Turn left

Gee Come, Haw Come—Turn right or left 180 degrees; used to reverse trail direction

Gee Over, Haw Over—Move to right or left side of trail

Trail—Request for right-of-way to pass another team

On By—Pass a trail junction, another team, or object of distraction

Hike—Start

Whoa—Stop

Line Out—Tighten gang line and hold it out

The terminology extends to the driver and team as well. The person who drives a dog team is a *musher;* to drive a team is to *mush;* and the sport of dog sledding is called *mushing.* The exact origin of the terms is unknown, but conjecture is they evolved from the French word *marcher,* meaning to march.

Napping in harness. (Joe Asarisi)

CARING FOR THE DOGS

A successful training program begins with healthy dogs. All vaccinations should be current and the dogs free of intestinal parasites. For dogs over 7 years of age or with a history of illness or injury, a complete veterinary examination is recommended prior to the start of training.

For top performance on the trail, a well-balanced diet is essential. Premium dog food is available in a variety of formulas for various activity levels. Although many competitive dog sledders supplement with meat during racing season, the

"Flat out." Though famed for endurance, the Siberian is really quite a fast dog, capable of speeds in harness of over 20 mph for several miles at a stretch. (Pat Shane)

nutritional needs of most dogs can be met with high-quality commercial food.

Early detection of a health problem can help keep a dog on the team all season. Learn to monitor each dog's performance and note any change in eating, drinking, or eliminating. Following each outing, check feet for cuts and tenderness, provide fresh water, and allow time for the dogs to cool down before packing to leave. If a team includes unspayed females, heat cycles are a concern. Unplanned breedings and aggression among males are two good reasons for in-season females to remain at home. Basic knowledge of canine first aid and emergency equipment repair is helpful. A roll of Vet Wrap™ for injuries and duct tape for repairs can solve a myriad of problems that may be encountered on the trail.

THE LURE OF COMPETITION

Dog sledding can be recreational or competitive in its focus, and although the goals differ, the two share training fundamentals. As the recreational driver gains experience, the lure of competition may become progressively harder to resist. To encourage participation in competitive events, dog clubs and race organizers offer junior and sportsman class divisions to introduce newcomers to competition.

Competitive dog sledding is divided into three categories—sprint, middle distance, and distance. The mileage in each category varies with geographical region, but the guideline is 5 to 30 miles for sprint, 50 to 350 miles for middle distance, and over 350 miles for distance.

Sprint has class divisions based on team size and mileage. The New England Sled Dog Club, formed in 1924, currently recommends the following:

Unlimited/Open—11 to 15 miles
Limited/8-Dog—8 to 11 miles
6-Dog Professional—3 to 8 miles
6-Dog Sportsman—3 to 8 miles
4-Dog Professional—3 to 4 miles
4-Dog Sportsman—3 to 4 miles
3-Dog Junior—3 to 4 miles
1-Dog Junior—¼ to 1 mile

(Unlimited/Open, Limited/8-Dog, and Professional classes compete for cash prizes; junior and sportsman compete for trophies.)

Already well-established in its own right, middle distance is increasing in popularity as its longer races become the "training grounds" for distance teams. A middle distance team consists of six or more dogs, with the exact number for each race determined by officials based on mileage and difficulty of terrain. A six-dog race which has become a favorite of purebred Siberian teams is New Hampshire's Sandwich Notch Sixty.

Held each February, the race is dedicated to the memory of Eva "Short" Seeley, who, with her husband Milton, operated Chinook Kennels in Wonalancet. The race course follows many of the area's historic dog sled trails where teams trained for Admiral Byrd's Antarctic expeditions and the U.S. Army's Search and Rescue Units.

GETTING STARTED

Before cool temperatures signal the start of training, schedule veterinary checks, become familiar with the equipment, and define realistic goals for the season based on the team's ability and amount of time allocated for training. Climate and trail conditions must also be considered when developing a training program. Will a wheeled rig be used all season, or only for early training? Are the trails flat, wide, and straight, or hilly and narrow with curves? Will the sled trails be set, or must the team break trail? A successful training program must be geared to what will be expected of the team and what it is realistically capable of achieving.

When the temperature falls below 60°F and the air is less humid, rig training can begin. There is a

All it takes is one kid and one Siberian to start a lifelong hobby. (Cheryl Scheall)

simple formula for determining if conditions are acceptable. Add the degrees of temperature to the percentage of relative humidity. If the sum does not exceed 110, conditions are cool enough that the dogs will not be easily susceptible to overheating.

For those anxious to begin training, an excellent early fall activity is hiking with dogs in harness. This accustoms puppies and inexperienced dogs to the feel of a harness and the action of pulling. Intersecting trails are ideal for training gee/haw leaders and testing the potential of young dogs. Hitch one or two dogs to the lead section of a gang line or a length of polyethylene rope with brass snaps; attach the other end to a wide belt worn by the hiker. Do not hike with more than two dogs for, without a mechanical means of braking, even two can be difficult to handle on hilly or rough terrain.

Wheeled rigs should be used on dirt or gravel surfaces; pavement is too rough on the dogs' feet and may cause injuries that will plague the team all season. Begin rig training with a small team, four or fewer dogs, over short distances, gradually adding miles. Transferring from a rig to the dog sled will require more adjustment for the driver

As an alternative to the more labor-intensive sled driving, and requiring fewer dogs, the sport of "skijoring" is enjoying a steady increase in popularity. (Bob Cleary)

than the dogs. Strength, balance, and endurance are needed to control the sled, ride the runners, and run alongside the sled on uphill sections of a trail. Once on the sled, both distance and speed will quickly increase.

Like their human counterparts, canine athletes must gradually attain a high level of fitness. Dick Moulton, chief dog trainer and handler at Chinook Kennels and on Admiral Byrd's 1939–41 Antarctic Expedition, advises running the dogs at least once every three days during the first six weeks of training when they are building muscle. This will prevent muscle loss caused by extended layoffs. "Early

A muddy day on the wheel rig. (Cheryl Scheall)

on, don't stress speed," warns Moulton, "it will come with more training. A dog must have a desire to run, "guts" as Moulton calls it, and no dog can be forced to perform beyond its capability. "I've seen many a dog," recalls Moulton, "whose desire to run was so strong that it overcame physical shortcomings to become a good sled dog."

Never too young to learn. (Virginia Hartranft)

A successful dog sledder builds individual relationships with the dogs. Jean Bryar, winner of six Women's North American Championships, credits her success to knowing her dogs so well, that she could predict how each dog would run on a particular day by the way it left the dog box. She knew who to run and who to leave off the team.

Excessive noise, tangled lines and dogs that chew are concerns for both experienced and novice dog sledders. The noise level created by the dogs while they are waiting to be hitched to the gang line often alarms beginners. As soon as the team is released, the only sound will be the sled gliding across the snow. Tangled lines are a frequent problem. Some dogs do learn to free themselves, but more often, the team must be stopped, the snow hook set, and the dogs untangled. If a dog must be unhitched from the gang line, do not unfasten the neck and tug lines simultaneously and risk a loose dog. Dogs that love to chew can be a serious problem on the trail. While a cable picket and gang line help to discourage chewing, nylon web collars and harnesses can be destroyed in seconds. If a team includes chewers, try to break the habit with continued reprimands and carry a spare collar and harness in the sled bag.

Dog sledding has three cardinal rules:

1. Always be in control. This means the driver, not the dogs, set the course.

2. Never let the brush bow hit the wheel dogs. The brush bow is the extension at the front of the sled. A driver must constantly keep the line to the sled tight, braking when necessary, to prevent the sled from hitting the dogs from behind.

3. Never let go of the sled. When the sled spills, it and the dogs will continue down the trail, with or without the driver. Unless there is a real danger of personal injury, try to hold on and regain control.

Training will have its good and not-so-good days. A dog sledder must learn to recognize when something is hindering the team's performance

Coming at you: Bill Leonard on the runners behind some of his Willo Siberians.

and be flexible in the training program to allow for adjustments. As the old saying goes, "A chain is only as strong as its weakest link." In dog sledding, it translates, "A team is only as fast as its slowest dog," but Charles Belford put it best, "Always train to the ability of your weakest dog."

The sport of dog sledding requires, above all, common sense. Becoming a proficient recreational or competitive driver will take time, patience, and a good sense of humor, but the reward for all the hard work can be enjoyed on the trail season after season.

OUTFITTERS

Please refer to the listing of outfitters for sledding equipment, that appears in the "Additional Resources—Books and Organizations" section at the end of this book.

BIBLIOGRAPHY

Fishback, Lee. *Training Lead Dogs*. Nunica, MI: Tun-Ora, 1978.

Flanders, Noel K. *The Joy of Running Sled Dogs*. Loveland, CO: Apline Publication, 1989.

The International Siberian Husky Club. *The Siberian Husky*. Elkhorn, WI: Spake Printing Services, Inc., 1994.

Additional Publications

Mushing
P.O. Box 149
Ester, AK 99725

Mush with P.R.I.O.E.—Sled Dog Care Guidelines
P.O. Box 84915
Fairbanks, AK 99708

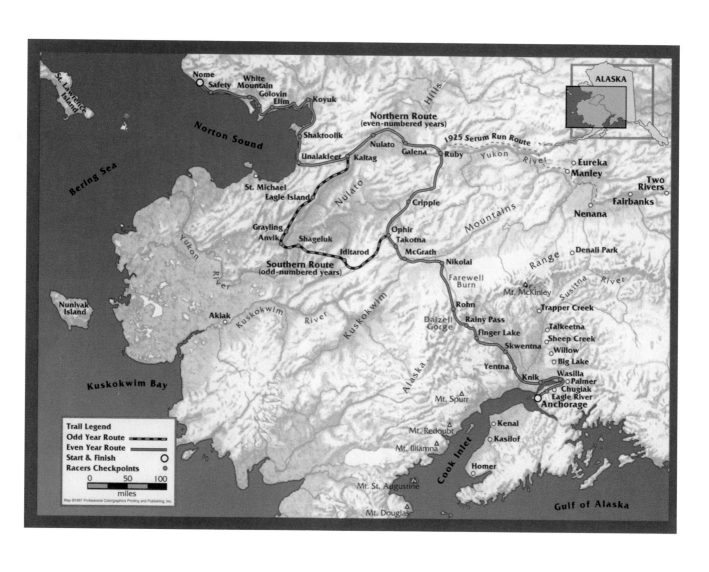

ALASKA

Nome
Safety
White
Mountain
Golovin
Elim
Koyuk

Norton Sound

Bering Sea

St. Lawrence Island

Shaktoolik

Northern Route
(even-numbered years)

1925 Serum Run Route

Nulato
Unalakleet
Kaltag
Galena
Ruby

Yukon
River

Eureka
Manley

Two
Rivers

St. Michael
Eagle Island

Cripple

Fairbanks

Nenana

Grayling
Anvik
Shageluk
Iditarod

Ophir
Takotna
McGrath

Mountains

Range

Denali Park

Southern Route
(odd-numbered years)

Nikolai

Yukon
River

Farewell
Burn

Mt. McKinley

Susitna
River

Nunivak
Island

Akiak

Kuskokwim   River

Kuskokwim

Rohn

Dalzell
Gorge

Rainy Pass

Finger Lake

Skwentna

Alaska

Trapper Creek

Talkeetna
Sheep Creek
Willow
Big Lake

Kuskokwim Bay

Yentna

Knik

Wasilla
Palmer
Chugiak
Eagle River
Anchorage

Mt. Spurr

Kenai

Mt. Redoubt

Kasilof

Mt. Iliamna

Cook Inlet

Homer

Mt. St. Augustine

Mt. Douglas

Gulf of Alaska

Trail Legend
Odd Year Route
Even Year Route
Start & Finish
Racers Checkpoints

0   50   100
miles

Map ©1997 Professional Colorgraphics Printing and Publishing, Inc.

CHAPTER 11

The Iditarod: *"The Last Great Race"*

Established in 1973 to commemorate the famous "Serum Run" of 1925, the annual Iditarod Trail Sled Dog Race, held the first Saturday in March, is a fixture of the Alaskan experience. Starting in Anchorage, it traverses the daunting Alaska mountain range and 1,100 miles of rugged, desolate tundra before ending in Nome on the Bering Sea coast. It is an incredibly grueling challenge for dogs and drivers, especially drivers. However, it does give the hardiest Siberian enthusiasts a chance to show that their dogs still exhibit the capacity, cited by the Standard, to pull "a light load at moderate speeds over tremendous distances." All-Siberian teams do not win the Iditarod, but they do compete credibly. As Iditarod musher, Wayne Curtis, writes,

> *Racing an all-Siberian team in the Iditarod is different than running a mixed-breed or Alaskan Husky team. Siberian Huskies are masters at conserving energy. With their thick undercoat and medium length guard hairs, they run best when it is very cold, and they use fewer calories to stay warm while resting. By running at a moderate speed, they can run longer with less rest. They are able to use their food more efficiently, so they carry fewer provisions on the trail. Siberian Huskies also have the ideal foot type to travel in snow and ice and have less need for protective booties. The temperament of the Siberian also makes for enjoyable companionship on the trail as you can always count on them to do the unexpected.*

What follows is an account of one Siberian musher's Iditarod experiences, along with photos of Wayne's own team on the trail in 1995 when he set a new record for time by an all-Siberian team. To the breed's great credit, that team included a number of competitive show Siberians, including the dog that would win Best of Opposite Sex at the 1998 National Specialty over an entry of nearly 1,350 animals.

EXPERIENCES ALONG THE IDITAROD TRAIL

BY PETER JOHNSON, DECEMBER 1998

I bought my first serious dogsled from a part-time carpenter and full-time sheep farmer in Vermont. I remember when I picked up the new sled that it seemed awfully large. My experience had been with sprint sleds that I used at infrequent snow races in southern New England. As I eyed the new sled, the old Yankee farmer must have sensed what I was thinking. "You need a tough sled like this. Maybe someday you'll run the Iditarod." Fat chance, I thought. Who would have thought that his words would turn out to be prophetic.

Several years later, in 1992, I had the great fortune to compete in the 1,150-mile Iditarod Trail Sled Dog Race across Alaska. The Iditarod is the most famous and longest of all sled dog races. In the late 1980s, it became known as *"that race in Alaska that a woman always wins."* Libby Riddles was the first woman to win in 1985 when she was the only musher, man or woman, to brave a terrible

Pete Johnson at the starting line of the 1992 Iditarod Sled Dog Race with his leader dog, Curly. (Steve Serafin)

snowstorm in the final stretch. Four-time champion Susan Butcher followed with several additional victories. This led to extensive television coverage, which further cemented the Iditarod's reputation as the world's premier sled dog race.

The Iditarod follows a meandering trail across three mountain ranges through the interior of Alaska. It begins in downtown Anchorage, Alaska's largest city with a population of about 300,000. Despite the hoopla supplied by several thousand spectators at the beginning, the Iditarod is truly a wilderness experience. After leaving the outskirts of the Anchorage area, mushers enter a wild country where there are no roads, no cars, and no modern conveniences. Once the race begins, the musher and his dog team are on their own. There is no handler support at all in the Iditarod. During the race, there is no access at all to the teams for spectators or handlers, except by charter aircraft. This makes the race more challenging, but it also makes the experience a great adventure.

The Beginning

My wife Donna and I got involved in mushing through our love of dogs, not racing. We acquired our first Siberian Husky puppy in 1981. We both loved northern dog breeds and debated about getting a Siberian Husky or an Alaskan Malamute. At the time, I had just joined a new software business started by fellow graduate students and faculty members from the Yale computer science department. Since we lived in a condominium, we decided to get the smaller breed of the two. That's how we ended up with Siberians. We were well on the way to becoming a typical YUPPIE couple in southern Connecticut.

Wayne Curtis with two members of his all-Siberian record-breaking 1995 team. On viewer's right is Ch. Stormwatch's Montana, CD (Monte), one of nine leaders on that team and also the BOS winner at the 1998 Siberian Husky Club of America Specialty over an entry of nearly 1,350 Siberians. (Joe Asarisi)

Everything changed forever one bright Sunday morning in early autumn. We were enjoying brunch at a fashionable restaurant in New Haven while reading the Sunday paper. Donna came across a short feature in the local section about a sled dog demonstration that was to be held that afternoon in a nearby town. The event was sponsored by the Connecticut Valley Siberian Husky Club. "Look at those dogs in the picture," Donna said. "They look just like our new puppy. Let's go!" And off we went. Nothing has been the same since.

When people ask me how I got involved in mushing, I always answer "one dog at a time." As it turns out, the pattern that has evolved for our lifestyle is typical of many mushing families. You start out with an opportunity to sled a family pet that you dearly love, as we did on that fateful afternoon in Connecticut. You make several new friends and have an absolute blast! You are amazed to learn that dog mushing is alive and well throughout the U.S. and the rest of the world. Before long, you get introduced to a wide network of "crazy" people, who seem to talk about nothing but dogs.

We began many new friendships in those early days, friendships that continue to this today. I was introduced to long-distance mushing by our good friends George and Ann Cook in the mid-1980s. I ran George's second string team in several 60-mile races and discovered that I preferred cross-country dog mushing to so-called sprint racing. Our rule of thumb to this day is simple: *Avoid races where it takes longer to drive to the event than it does to compete.*

Of course, everyone eventually wants to run his or her own team. Slowly but surely, we acquired more and more dogs so that we could run bigger and bigger teams in longer and longer races. Today, our kennel averages about thirty Siberian Huskies (and one Belgian Sheepdog). Since I travel frequently on business, Donna manages the kennel and takes primary responsibility for the dogs' day-to-day care. Often she claims that the one sheepdog is more trouble than all of the Huskies put together. (Sorry Tucker.)

Ah . . . Alaska!

It is interesting to note that most people who develop an interest in northern dog breeds and dog mushing eventually find their way to Alaska. Our first trip to the Frontier State was in late summer of 1986. There we met Earl and Natalie Norris, who (to the best of my knowledge) operate the longest-running racing kennel in the world. At the time, the Norrises had nearly 200 dogs living on their farm in Willow, Alaska. Earl hooked up fourteen dogs and took me for a hairraising ride on his wheeled training cart (which was actually an old car chassis).

Personally, I think Earl secretly likes to scare tourists. On me, it had the opposite effect. I was absolutely amazed. Here was a team of dogs that had been bred for generations to perform in harness. The dogs were strong, fast, and incredibly powerful. I decided on the spot that this was the type of dog I'd like to develop in my kennel. Donna and I have focused our breeding program around Anadyr Dogs ever since. (Anadyr is the prefix used by Earl and Natalie Norris in naming dogs. Their official name is Alaskan Kennels, which is sometimes called the Howling Dog Farm. The Norris' live in Willow, Alaska, which is about 90 minutes north of Anchorage.)

It wasn't only the dogs that had a profound impact on me during that trip. Alaska is a beautiful yet wild place. The land is rugged and unconventional, and so are the people. The Norris household is no exception. It was (and remains) a common meeting place for dog mushers from throughout the region. In the course of that memorable afternoon visit, we met many famous Iditarod competitors who stopped by to chat, and to buy dog food from Earl's son, J. P.

Several years later, some of our friends were touring Alaska during the summer. They hit all the major attractions from the Southeast to Fairbanks. It seems that no matter where they stopped, they came across a placard, a postcard, or some sort of memorabilia featuring Earl and Natalie Norris.

When they later met us and the Norrises for dinner, they remarked that they must be in the presence of greatness. Earl and Natalie truly are an integral part of the history of Alaska. I could have acquired no better mentors to introduce me to the sport of long-distance mushing.

After our first visit to Alaska in 1986, Donna and I just couldn't stay away. They say that nobody should visit Alaska when they are young, because every other destination will pale by comparison. For us, it wasn't an issue because we kept going back. In 1989, Donna spent the entire winter with the Norrises as an apprentice. I was fortunate to join Donna at the dog farm for six weeks over the holidays and early January. This happened to be one of the coldest winters in Alaskan history. I remember that Donna and I literally used to go into the outdoor walk-in freezer to warm up.

During that visit, Earl and Natalie gave me the opportunity to run one of their teams in the Knik 200, an Iditarod qualifier race. In Alaska, this race is casually referred to as a mid-distance race. At the drivers' meeting the trail boss said there would be no trail crew because the race was so short! In the lower 48, we typically call a 60-mile race mid-distance. Anything longer is considered to be truly a marathon event. Nonetheless, I had a wonderful time. This was when I had the first inkling that mushing across Alaska might be something I could really enjoy.

Iditarod Season

Iditarod time at the Norris household is always exciting. I've been fortunate enough to be in

The excitement is obvious in this view of the start of the 1995 Iditarod. (Joe Asarisi)

Alaska for several Iditarods. The race is even more exciting when you personally know some of the competitors. It was after observing various mushers prepare for the race at the Norrises' that I first had the notion that I could run the race myself.

Earl and Natalie have mentored many Iditarod mushers over the years, including multiple-champion Martin Buser, who went on to establish his own kennel in Alaska. For Siberian Husky lovers, it is particularly exciting when Norris dogs (or other purebred teams) are competing. As the race draws near, the extended Norris household goes into full gear preparation. There are food drops and components of extra sledding equipment to be shipped. Sleds must be put in top condition. Dogs must be vaccinated, wormed, and tuned into top condition. And the mushers, with Earl and Natalie's input, prepare a final race strategy in which periods of rest and running are scheduled.

After several months of preparation, the entire effort comes to a head during Iditarod week. For first-time Iditarod mushers, there is a mandatory rookie meeting early in the week. This is followed by an all-day driver meeting at which last-minute trail conditions are reviewed in detail. Two days before the race, there is a huge banquet in Anchorage. Mushers sign autographs, have photographs taken, and draw starting positions. On Saturday, the ceremonial start begins in downtown Anchorage. After a brief 25-mile run to Eagle River, the dogs are trucked to Wasilla where the race begins in earnest.

After the restart, the Iditarod is truly a wilderness race, and the mushers are on their own. (The restart is held at various villages in the Matanuska valley, depending on snow conditions. Wasilla and Willow are the most common points of departure.) There are no roads to the checkpoints. Handlers can't follow the teams or provide any assistance whatsoever. However, for a mushing fan, it is all very exciting. The news media provides frequent updates as the race progresses. Volunteers man the phones at race headquarters to answer questions from around the world about each musher's position. In more recent years, a number of web sites have also popped up to provide extensive race coverage.

Preparation

What the fans don't see are the months of preparation that are required to bring a team to the starting line. We decided to run the Iditarod nearly two years prior to actually competing. Running a 1,000-mile-plus dogsled race is not something you can do casually. As the senior technology officer of a small software company, I had to arrange and plan for an extended leave of absence. We also had to make extensive financial preparations. Fortunately, I got the help of a good friend, Bill Hahn, who arranged several fund-raising events leading up to the race. Bill was the musher who first introduced us to sled dogs back on that fateful afternoon in Connecticut. Here he was, several years later, helping me get to the starting line of the Iditarod. One never knows what fate will bring.

Donna and I decided to make arrangements with Earl and Natalie to run one of their teams in the Iditarod. By that time, we also had some dogs of our own that we thought could compete. However, we realized that our chances for success were much greater if we could leverage the talents of dogs that had already been to Nome. We decided to fly to Alaska for the winter rather than try to transport our kennel on the ground. This saved me from taking several additional weeks off from work.

Since running the Iditarod is such a spectacularly unique event, I decided to involve the entire community. The Governor of New Hampshire wrote me a letter of felicitation to deliver to the people of Nome. Children from our small elementary school in Webster, New Hampshire, wrote letters that I delivered to school children in remote Alaskan villages along the way. I flew the flag of New Hampshire from my sled at both the start and the end of the race. I also made arrangements to raise funds for the New Hampshire Chapter of the March of Dimes. Starting with the Governor (now Senator Judd Gregg), citizens pledged and donated funds for every mile that I completed along the Iditarod trail.

All of these arrangements were put into motion several months prior to the race. Finally, in late September of 1991, it was time to move to Alaska for the final stage of our adventure. Donna and I loaded up about a half dozen dogs, placed several others with friends, and headed to Alaska. By coincidence, we met Iditarod Champion Joe Runyun on the final leg of our journey. Joe gave me some good advice: to rest the dogs a little more than you run them. This turned out to be a good formula for ensuring a successful completion of the race.

Life at the Howling Dog Farm

Earl and Natalie picked us up at the airport in Anchorage in the middle of the night. The next day, we were running dogs on wheels. Earl had been training a pool of about twenty-five dogs all summer. This group came to be known as the Iditarod dogs. By the time I arrived, the dogs were already starting to get in condition. We were off to a good start.

The winter of 1991–92 was a spectacular season for mushing. By mid-October, the first snowstorm came and we ran on sleds from there on out. Before long, Donna and I were training three teams of dogs, ranging in size from seven to nine dogs. Earl always said that running smaller teams really toughens up the dogs, which I still feel is good advice.

One thing we did learn early on was that not all of the rules about mushing apply equally to Siberian Huskies. We went to the Alaska Dog Mushers Association (ADMA) meeting in Fairbanks that year and heard several famous mushers speak about nutrition. I was amazed to learn that typical Alaskan Husky teams consume upwards of 8,000 calories a day (or more) toward the end of the Iditarod. Later, I discovered that I couldn't realistically feed my dogs more than about 4,500 calories. Yet they didn't lose weight, even under extremely cold conditions. Siberian Huskies have been bred for centuries to be fuel-efficient, a characteristic that has been lost in modern sled dogs, who are bred more for speed than efficiency. In today's racing environment, there is little advantage to fuel efficiency. But, obviously, this was historically very important for survival.

As the winter progressed, we developed a pattern of running each dog three days on, one day off. On a typical day, our training runs ranged from eight miles to thirty miles. Most of the time, we ran directly out of Earl and Natalie's property in Willow, though we occasionally trekked the dogs to other areas for the sake of variation.

One afternoon we were running two teams in Big Lake on the Iditarod trail. After many miles of running, we stopped the teams along the trail to practice using a new cooker. A few minutes later, along comes a very fast team of Alaskan Huskies driven by a very attractive young woman. When she got closer, I saw that it was 1995 Iditarod Champion Libby Riddles. Libby was out on a fun run. She stopped to chat for awhile and share some cookies. Libby is an extremely popular figure in Alaska and is an excellent spokesperson for dog mushing. She really makes you feel welcome, even when you are a rookie musher who is camping too close to the trail.

Life that year at the Howling Dog Farm was good. We made many new friends and got lots of good advice from the Willow mushing community. As the apprentice of Earl Norris, it seemed that I was welcome everywhere I went. When we weren't training and caring for the dogs, we enjoyed long conversations with Earl and Natalie. We learned about the history of dogsledding in Alaska and the history of our breed.

The 1991 holiday season was absolutely beautiful. People always ask what it's like to deal with the long hours of darkness during early winter. What they don't realize is that the bright moonlight and aurora borealis in Alaska are more spectacular than common sunlight. One night before Christmas, we all decided to go caroling by dog team. From the Norris property, there is an extensive trail system that connects to several neighboring houses. Natalie helped me make moose-shaped Christmas cookies that we loaded into sleds to deliver to our neighbors. The night was crisp and clear with bright moonlight as we mushed off into the forest without headlamps.

Soon we arrived at our first neighbor's house, which was about ten miles away. By then the cookies were in pieces, but nobody seemed to care. We tied up the dog teams and made a lame attempt to sing a Christmas carol. The neighbor invited us in and offered refreshments. (I think she would have done anything to stop the singing.) To our surprise, the table was all set with lots of goodies, as if she had been expecting us. After being out in the cold, everyone was hungry so we made quick work of the food and beer. Shortly thereafter, another neighbor arrived (by car), who was all dressed up. I realized then that we had inadvertently interrupted a Christmas dinner party. But we had already eaten all the food, left nothing but broken cookies, and the dogs were beginning to howl. Nonetheless, everyone was in good cheer. We eventually made our way home by dog team with another new memory and some even closer friendships.

Time for Serious Training

After the holidays, I lengthened our training runs and began to sort out which dogs would make the team. Donna helped me evaluate dogs by completing several long runs herself. To this end, she completed her own Iditarod qualifier, the Knik 200 race in early January. Donna took several young dogs whose endurance was questionable. By running them 200 miles, she was able to spot dogs that could be problematic for the Iditarod. She also became the backup Iditarod musher in case something would happen to me. Despite the fact that she had the flu and stayed far too long at the halfway checkpoint, Donna did quite well. The race was a success and gave me added confidence in my team.

I also went on a few camping trips with some friends. On one particularly cold weekend, I was joined by Scott Cameron, an old friend that has successfully completed the Iditarod, the Yukon Quest, and the Hope race. These are the three longest races in the world. Scott and I mushed teams to Yentna station, about 75 miles from the Knik bar where we started. I wanted to test out my gear (and Scott is just plain nuts about mushing), so we slept outside with the dogs in temperatures of about −30°F. It was a brilliantly clear night and we witnessed one of the most spectacular displays of the aurora borealis I have ever seen. It was magnificent. I survived and got my first taste of what it would be like living along the trail during the Iditarod.

I also began to prepare my food drops for the race. The Iditarod has about twenty checkpoints. Mushers ship out about a ton of supplies, mostly dog food, for use during the race. It took me weeks to cut meat and fish into small pieces to be fed out during the race. I sent out fish, beef, chicken, fat, turkey skins, and lamb. I sent out high-quality dry dog food, extra batteries, and food for myself. In Alaska, meat for sled dogs is readily available in mushing specialty stores. J. P. Norris, Earl's son, runs Underdog Feeds, one of the premier mushing supply stores in the Anchorage area. J. P. and his wife Kari (herself a two-time Iditarod musher) were tremendous supporters. J. P. managed to secure for me about a ton of salmon, beautiful filets that were destined for upscale tourist restaurants in Anchorage. Apparently, they had been in a truck that had temporarily lost refrigeration and could no longer be guaranteed for human consumption. (Yes, I ate some myself, and it was delicious.) Kari sewed my sled bag, my parka, and most of my dog booties.

Many other Siberian Husky fanciers in the Willow area helped me as well. Dave Totten, noted Alaskan artist, helped train dogs with me and produced many fine photographs and pieces of art. His wife Barb made all of my food for the race. Earl's other son, Ted Norris, helped me mount a dog box onto an old truck that we borrowed. The other dog handlers at the Norris house, Albert Beattie, Maureen Chrysler, and Sharon Wiloshen, also helped me train dogs. It was truly a team effort to get me to the Iditarod starting line.

Getting myself into shape was not difficult. Running dogs outside in below-zero temperatures every day will definitely take excess weight off any musher. After the holidays, I also gave up beer and caffeine. I was determined to be as helpful to the team as I could be by the time the race started.

As the day of the race approached, I was still up in the air about which dog would be the fifteenth on my team. In 1992, mushers were allowed to take up to twenty dogs on their team. I had, however, decided that fifteen dogs would be enough for me. I had a number of dogs that had already completed the race, including Curley, my primary lead dog. I was running Siberian Huskies, after all. I reasoned that even if they weren't faster, they were tougher than most of the dogs that would be competing. In the end, I believe that I made the right decision. I started with fewer dogs than any other musher and I finished with more (thirteen of fifteen). Siberian Huskies are made for this stuff. By the way, the last dog I chose, big ol' Hoss, made it all the way to Nome.

The Race Approaches

Finally, after many months of preparation, the big day was approaching. The final week was nothing but a blur. I had several visitors (mostly Siberian Husky fanciers) arrive from throughout the lower 48, including my father and mother. My mother had been quite ill for some time. This was the last long trip she was able to make before she died. It meant a lot to have her there. My dad had been an incredibly successful football coach in the small midwest town where I grew up. He knew just what to say to give me gentle encouragement before the race.

George Cook and family arrived during a snowstorm on the night of the banquet, two days before the race. George had just completed the Yukon Quest, and had forgone postrace celebrations to rush back to see me off in Anchorage. He delivered the New Hampshire flag, which he had carried on his sled the 1,000 miles from Fairbanks to White Horse. The flag was passed on to my sled bag, where it would continue its journey from Anchorage to Nome.

Both Quest mushers and Iditarod mushers faced extremely cold weather that year, with temperatures frequently dipping below -50°F. In retrospect, it seems funny now, but at the time the sight of George was a bit frightening. George's face was still recovering from frostbite and he lost quite a bit of weight during the race. He basically had no butt. It was a wonder he could keep his pants up. I could see the look of concern on my mother's face when she saw George. At the banquet, I was too nervous to eat much and several members of our party had not been able to make it due to the snowstorm. George proceeded to eat about five steak dinners that night and he still looked hungry. Was this what I had to look forward to?

The snowstorm continued up to the morning of the race. Usually, snow gets trucked into downtown Anchorage to cover the streets for the start. In 1992, this wasn't necessary. Mother Nature provided fresh snow for the occasion. I stayed with my parents in their hotel room the night before the race, hoping I could get some sleep. Fat chance. Donna stayed back at the dog farm and helped the crew bring the dogs to Anchorage early Saturday morning. This in itself was an adventure when the truck wouldn't start. Eventually the crew members got it going at around 4 A.M. the next day and made their way to Anchorage with the dogs and the starting sleds. The snowstorm continued until just before the race got underway.

The Day of the Start

It had been nearly two years since I began planning for this adventure. Countless hours of training and preparation were now behind me. The big day had finally arrived. Today, I would begin the Iditarod, the longest race in the world. In even-numbered years, the race is run along a northern route that spans about 1,150 miles. I was about to begin a very long journey.

Negotiating the first turn after the start—with drag sled and passenger. (Joe Asarisi)

To gain confidence, I had mushed most of the first few hundred miles in training. This part of the trail would be familiar to me. Nonetheless, Donna says she has never seen me so nervous. Friends at the staging area surrounded me. Kathleen, the Cooks' 4-year-old daughter, rode in the basket as everyone helped me to the starting line. Lead dog Curley proudly moved forward in single lead. He had been here before and he knew what he was doing. Bill Hahn rode my drag sled between Anchorage and Eagle River, which took about three hours. I really don't remember much about this stretch, except that there were crowds everywhere. My real fun would begin once I left civilization.

In those days, you were competing as soon as you left Anchorage. The rules have since been changed and the first day no longer counts. (This is one of the reasons times in recent years have been so much faster.) I'm not sure I like the new system better. Now the musher has two sleepless nights before the race really begins.

After arriving in Eagle River, the dogs are trucked to the restart in Wasilla, which begins four hours later. Again, competing mushers left the starting line pulling a drag sled to the next checkpoint in Knik, about fifteen miles away. That's where the real wilderness race begins. My good friend Steve Serafin rode my drag sled to the Knik Bar, which serves as the checkpoint. It is also famous for its wild party during the start of the Iditarod. Steve and I had mushed and played together for years in New England. It had always been his dream to mush a dog team to a bar. Now he was finally getting his chance in the Iditarod.

When we reached the checkpoint, I put on my expedition clothing and switched the dogs from the ceremonial sled to the wilderness sled. I also donned a sidearm. The area ahead was famous for being moose-infested. I kissed my mother and my wife good-bye. From here on, I would get no assistance until I reached Nome. The race for me was about to begin.

On the Iditarod Trail

Sleeping with the Moose

All of the Iditarod veterans I had talked to warned me that the first day is the toughest. This is absolutely true. All of the hoopla at the beginning has an exhausting effect on both the mushers and the dogs. Once you get into a regular pattern of running, feeding, and resting, the race actually gets easier.

As I left the bar in Knik, my team was turbocharged. Fifteen dogs were no longer pulling a drag sled and extra passenger. The sled must have felt like a feather to them. We were nearly out of control as we whipped around trees, around other teams, and off into the wilderness.

My plan when I left Knik was to mush to Flat Horn Lake (about thirty miles) and give the dogs a good meal and four hours of rest. I would then mush on to

Heading toward first checkpoint. (Joe Asarisi)

Skwentna, which was about another seventy miles away. I looked forward to this as an easy part of the journey. After all, I knew all of these trails very well. Unfortunately, the snowstorm had blown most of them in and made for very tough going.

As I approached Flat Horn, I saw Norman Vaughn, a famous musher who was then in his mid-80s. I watched Norman expertly pull his team off the trail and settle them down to rest. It took him about two minutes to do what I managed to do in twenty; experience makes all the difference. When I reached the lake, I settled my team down

and fed them. Food and water were fresh from my cooler so it wasn't necessary to build a fire. It was about -20°F and for the first time in about three days, after taking care of the dogs, I settled myself on the sled to get a brief nap.

About two hours later, I woke up shivering. It was just before sunrise and the temperature had dropped dramatically. As the sun came up, I noticed several moose running down the trail ahead of me. I could see where they had bedded down nearby. Knik's reputation for moose is well-deserved. In any event, they posed no threat as they were moving away from me. However, as soon as the dogs saw them I could hardly hold the team back.

It is quite commonplace in Alaska for mushers to encounter moose, although it's usually not a problem. After a while, the moose usually just move away. However, in years when the snow is very deep, moose prefer to travel on packed dog/snowmobile trails. Sometimes, when they see a dog team coming toward them, they get angry. It is as if they feel the team is encroaching on their

Crossing the Finger Lake checkpoint in the Alaska Range. (Joe Asarisi)

Apparently, some of the dogs had gotten very sick and it was going to be necessary to scratch. I felt heartbroken for the musher. After all that preparation, having to scratch at the beginning must be a nightmare come true. I felt lucky that all of my dogs were in good shape and I moved on. Several hours later, I arrived at Joe Delia's cabin, the checkpoint in Skwentna.

Pandemonium in Skwentna

Skwentna is the first village checkpoint in the race and one of the most popular locations for media coverage. So many airplanes fly over Skwentna during the Iditarod that special air traffic control arrangements must be made to insure safety in the skies. There seemed to be dog teams everywhere as I entered the checkpoint.

trail. On such occasions, moose have been known to attack dog teams and their mushers.

The best-known incident occurred during the 1995 Iditarod when Susan Butcher's team was attacked by moose in the Knik area. Several dogs were severely injured and others were killed. Since then, most mushers carry weapons to protect their teams. I've had several moose encounters over the years while mushing in Alaska. I've even had moose jump over my lead dogs. Fortunately, I've never had an encounter that ended badly for either the moose or my team.

As I made my way to Rabbit Lake and Skwentna, I came across a musher in trouble.

After bedding down and feeding my dogs, I walked up to the checkpoint cabin. This is one of the many places along the trail that is notorious for outstanding hospitality. The place was packed with wall-to-wall mushers enjoying the fine spread of food laid out by the Delias. The tough trail had taken its toll. Unbelievably, several mushers were taking their mandatory 24-hour layover in Skwentna, which is only 150 miles from the start! "The trail's blown over out there. No point in going on until the weather improves." I heard one veteran musher exclaim.

I wasn't sure what to do. I had planned to rest for six hours at this checkpoint and continue

The driver depends on dogs working harmoniously together. (Joe Asarisi)

get down the trail and stick to your plan." Emit told me. After a few hours rest on the river with my dogs, I did as I was told.

Emit was absolutely right. The weather cleared and the temperature got very cold. Best of all, the trail conditions ahead were nearly perfect. The dogs flew down the trail as we approached the mountain range ahead. I couldn't believe after 150 miles that the dogs could still lope so fast! I was ecstatic.

The Happy River and Rainy Pass

I rested during the middle part of the day at the next checkpoint in Finger Lake, a simple tent site in the middle of nowhere. Race veterinarians checked out my entire team and pronounced every dog very fit. I was particularly concerned about the dogs' feet at this point because the weather was so cold. The dogs had been wearing booties for protection from the very beginning. However, the constant friction of moving down the trail in these conditions can still cause problems. So far, all the dogs were fine.

I dreaded the next part of the trail, the Happy River crossing, which presents what is probably the toughest sled handling on the Iditarod. As Earl describes it, "You'll be mushing along this giant river gorge. You can't believe the trail could possibly drop down onto this river, you're so far above it. You just can't believe they'd put a trail in there. But all of the sudden, the trail goes off the side of a cliff and down you go. It's unbelievable!"

down the trail toward Nome. Should I stay longer because of the tough weather conditions? I was concerned that my dogs wouldn't get enough rest in this checkpoint because it was so crowded. On the other hand, I didn't want to leave if I should really be taking my mandatory 24-hour.

Earl told me before the race that there were certain mushers that I should go to for advice if I needed it. One of these was former champion Emit Peters, a native musher from Ruby. Emit Peters was known as the "Yukon River Fox" for his crafty racing strategy. Earl and Emit were old friends, and I knew he was somebody to be trusted. I quietly approached Emit, introduced myself, and asked him what I should do. "Your dogs look fine and the weather will be fine. You

This is what a hardworking team looks like to the driver as the lead dogs reach the crest of a hill. (Joe Asarisi)

tree. By the time I got to the river gorge itself, I was exhausted from muscling my sled around obstacles. Fortunately, the snow was deep that year and I was able to successfully make my way down to the river without crashing. It's definitely the scariest trail I've ever been on. On the other side, you begin a very steep ascent on your way up to Rainy Pass.

Night began to fall, and with it the temperature. At this point, I suffered my most painful experience of the race. The cold temperatures and high winds caused one of my contact lenses to freeze to my eye. It felt like somebody was trying to gouge out my eyeball. I didn't get any relief until I could warm up at the next checkpoint, the Rainy Pass lodge. When I arrived, the place was so crowded that there was hardly a place to stand up (let alone sleep). So I ended up camping outside with my dogs. I stayed for several hours to get some much-needed rest for the dogs. Much of this time was spent tending to the dogs' feet. Some of them were beginning to get sore and medication was necessary. Both my dogs and I had suffered on that cold trip through the Happy River into Rainy Pass. Next, we could look forward to dropping down through the mountains in the notorious Dalzell Gorge.

The Dalzell Gorge, Rohn, and the Burn

I timed my departure from Rainy Pass so that I would enter the treacherous Dalzell Gorge during daylight. This is one of the scariest parts of the trail to many mushers. The trail literally drops over the top of the Alaska Range down a windy path that

Earl's description was mild compared to the real thing. For miles, the musher and team must negotiate narrow trails with lots of side hilling. More than once I found myself wrapped around a follows a streambed. At the bottom, you reach the convergence of the Rohn and Kuskokwim rivers.

At the top of the pass, I had my first experience with a crevasse. As I was passing over a particularly fresh snowy area, I looked down between my runners to see the trail disappear beneath me as I moved forward. I had crossed over a very deep crevasse and the weight of my sled was just enough to collapse the top layer. Fortunately, none of my dogs (or me) fell into the gaping hole.

When I began to drop down the gorge, my first reaction was: "This isn't too bad." I had done a lot of mushing in the White Mountains of New Hampshire and was used to dealing with steep terrain. There was plenty of snow and the trail was smooth and well-covered. An airplane flew overhead and took my picture. After the race, I learned that this photograph made

At McGrath, Alaska, team Stormwatch took the required 24-hour rest. (Joe Asarisi)

"Monte"(Ch. Stormwatch's Montana, CD) wearing red "wrist" wraps, enjoys a well-deserved rest. (Joe Asarisi)

the cover of the *Anchorage Daily News.*

Unfortunately, my luck didn't hold out. Somewhere about halfway down the gorge the trail began to wind back and forth around the stream. You would think that all the water would be frozen at temperatures that must have been about -25°F. This was not the case. Around one particularly sharp bend, I went over the side of the trail and into open water. The dogs managed to stay on the trail and were fine. However, I knew that it was absolutely critical for me to change my footgear immediately in order to survive. I managed to chop through my frozen boots and put on a backup set before my feet could freeze. Thank goodness I was prepared for this type of emergency.

Before long, I reached the Rohn checkpoint. This is nothing more than a small primitive cabin near the base of the river. However, it did have one

Pulling out to pass. (Joe Asarisi)

Do "six-legged" dogs run faster? The scene is Hatcher Pass, near Willow. (Joe Asarisi)

luxury that a musher could really look forward to in extremely cold weather. It had an outhouse!

At Rohn, I got a chance to observe some of the leading mushers. Everyone was taking a fairly long rest to prepare for the grueling 100-mile trek across the Burn to the next checkpoint. In particular, it was interesting to watch Rick Swenson care for his dogs. He was extremely efficient. He also didn't have a hair out of place. He looked like he had just started the race an hour ago. I, on the other hand, had developed a pretty bad case of frostbite on my face. I didn't take it personally when Beverly Masek, a well-known native American musher told me: "You've got to do something about your face." From then on, I was more careful to use the hood of my parka, which was equipped with a very good ruff.

After taking care of my dogs, I was fortunate to find a place next to Susan Butcher to sleep for a few hours inside the tiny cabin. This had to be one of the coldest periods of the race and I was grateful to be inside for awhile. I stayed way too long in Rohn, but I eventually got going again. My dogs and I were both well rested as we headed out toward the Burn and Nicolai.

The darkening sky over Hatcher Pass has a primal beauty all its own. (Joe Asarisi)

It's a "straight shot" as the team nears Big Lake. (Joe Asarisi)

The Burn is a long open stretch of land that was the site of a forest fire many years ago. It is notorious for being barren of snow, since it no longer has any tree coverage to block the wind. In 1992, however, I found this to be one of the easiest parts of the trail. I camped along the trail once, but soon found my way into Nicolai, a good-sized native village in the interior.

In the heart of Nicolai is a beautiful old Russian Orthodox church. The people there are warm and friendly. My eye was still in pretty bad shape and there were plenty of facilities and places to sleep. I decided that this was a good place to take my mandatory 24-hour rest. One of the race veterinarians, who was also an M.D., took a look at my sore eye. "You've scratched up the cornea pretty bad," he said, "but you should be okay in a few days. Probably you'll want to drop out of the race and fly back to the city to have an eye doctor take a look."

There was no way that I would ever consider dropping out of the race. My dog team was still in good shape. After so many months of preparation, I could deal with a little pain while my eye healed. As it turned out, I was back to normal in a few more days.

I did, unfortunately, drop one dog in Nicolai. He had developed very sore feet and this same veterinarian encouraged me (but didn't order me) to drop him. In retrospect, dropping this dog was probably a mistake. By the time the dog made it back to Anchorage a day or two later, he was fine. If I had been more experienced with this type of foot problem, I would have been able to nurse his feet back to health. I later learned that this veterinarian/M.D., the fellow who encouraged me to scratch, was on his first Iditarod mission. Furthermore, he was from Georgia! I should have found an Alaskan vet.

After twenty-four hours of rest, my dog team (now down to fourteen) acted like they were just starting a new race. Even after traveling nearly 400 miles, they were full of the devil. The local checkpoint workers helped me guide my team through the streets of Nicolai and out onto the trail. I tried to use my snow hook to slow the team down. Even though it was attached to the sled with aircraft cable, it wasn't strong enough. The cable broke and off we went at a gallop. This team was ready to go!

Ghosts in Ophir

The team traveled very well during the next part of the race, from Nikolai to McGrath, Takotna, and Ophir. Unbelievably, the weather got even colder. Wearing every piece of clothing I had in my sled, I chased a moose down the river into McGrath very early in the morning. Though I had donned a neoprene facemask to protect my nose, when I pulled into the checkpoint, I realized that all of the moisture in my nose had frozen anyway, leaving me with a big ice ball on my face. As I peeled off the mask, an outer layer of skin from my nose peeled off as well. I was so mad at the manufacturer that I vowed to send them a piece of my nose. Later I learned that temperatures that morning had dropped below -50°F.

Earl had flown into McGrath to meet me. The dogs were doing very well and were only scheduled for a 4-hour stop. After taking care of the team, I had just enough time to enjoy a brief breakfast with Earl before I was on my way again down the trail. It was great for me and the dogs to see our "coach," even if it was only for a short visit.

The next checkpoint, Takotna, is a small town only about twenty-five miles from McGrath. The team didn't really need a rest at that point, but Takotna is famous for its hospitality, so I dropped in for a quick lunch. The reputation of this checkpoint is well deserved. The people there were very generous. As I ate, I watched a weather forecast being broadcast on a small satellite television set. It looked like there could be heavy snow ahead. I hustled out the door and got my team moving to enjoy a fast trail as long as possible.

Ophir used to be a thriving mining village many years ago. Now it's just a ghost town. The terrain rises dramatically as you slowly make your

"Humping it" near Wasilla. Many trails test the determination of dogs and drivers. (Joe Asarisi)

before the checkpoint were the worst. As I sledded around several abandoned pieces of antique mining equipment, I could swear that I had been to this place before.

Some volunteers from Willow are kind enough to open up a house in Ophir every year to serve as the race checkpoint. The trail into town required the team to pass through a considerable amount of overflow, so the sled was covered with ice by the time I reached my resting spot. (Overflow is a layer of water that develops over a frozen lake or stream. Sometimes it is only a few inches thick, but sometimes it gets substantially deeper.) It took me about an hour to chip off the ice with my axe. Before long, it was time to move on. From Ophir, the race trail moves to the north in even-numbered years and south in odd-numbered years. The alternative routes converge again as they come off the Yukon River in Kaltag. Since it was 1992, I headed north to Cripple and Ruby as a light snow began to fall.

Traveling Together in the Wilderness

The Iditarod has far more checkpoints than the Yukon Quest, the other 1,000-mile race in the world of dog mushing. Consequently, teams are able to replenish their supplies more frequently and don't need to carry as much weight on their sled. However, fans back in Anchorage probably have the wrong idea about what these checkpoints are really like. Many are essentially wilderness stopovers with a tent or two and no other facilities. Cripple is a good example. This checkpoint is nothing but a tent site where mushers can resupply and rest for a

way up an old road that connects Takotna and Ophir. The views are spectacular. However, as it began to get dark, I had an incredibly eerie feeling. I felt like I was being watched. The last ten miles few hours on their way to the Yukon. In essence, Iditarod mushers travel about 175 miles in the wilderness between Ophir and Ruby.

At this point in the race, I had established a run/rest pattern of about six hours on, six hours off. During a typical 6-hour rest stop, I was sometimes able to get as much as an hour and a half of sleep. The remainder of the time is spent cooking for the dogs and caring for their feet, or any other physical needs that develop. The first rule of distance mushing is that the dogs must always come first.

The Cripple wilderness site is about half way through the race. By this time, dog teams that are traveling at a similar pace tend to group together. I was traveling in one of the middle groups that clearly wasn't in contention for any purse money. (In 1992, the purse was paid out to the first twenty mushers. There were seventy-six competitors that year, the largest field before or since.) This was a great opportunity to establish some strong friendships and enjoy trail camaraderie. From Cripple, I traveled together with Jim Oehschlaeger and Steve Christon all the way to Ruby. We took turns breaking trail, which provided some relief to all of our dogs.

At one point along the way, we all stopped to snack our dogs and check their feet, replacing dog booties as needed. We were all completely exhausted from lack of sleep. So we agreed to nap for ten minutes and then move on. Each musher lay down on top of his respective sled and closed his eyes. Two hours later I woke up from the sound of Jim's snoring. I rousted everyone and we moved on.

Down the Yukon River

It took over a day to travel the 115 miles to Ruby and we arrived in the middle of the night. Ruby is a beautiful village on the Yukon River and we were greeted with warm food and a soft place to sleep. After caring for our dogs and getting a few hours of rest, we three amigos moved on down the river. The Yukon is a huge river, over a mile wide in some spots.

The trail on the Yukon was quite smooth that year so there was no longer any advantage for the three teams to travel together. However, we still saw each other frequently both on the trail and in the checkpoints. As I arrived in the village of Nulato, I saw Jim being carted away to the medical center. He apparently had developed some pretty bad frostbite on his face and was having trouble with one of his eyes. Nevertheless, he was back on the trail later that day.

Sleep deprivation is one of the hardest things to get used to as an Iditarod musher. In a typical 24-hour period, any musher is lucky to get a total of two or three hours of sleep. A continuous stretch of four hours of sleep is a real luxury. After days of this, many mushers suffer from hallucinations. I chatted about this with some of my fellow mushers in Kaltag, the last checkpoint on the Yukon River. "I went around that last bend in the river," one musher said, "and I saw the Waltons standing on the shore waving to me." "That's nothing," another musher quipped, "I saw the Flintstones waving at me!" I felt fortunate that I didn't react this way to lack of sleep.

Across the Tundra to the Coast

After my dogs were fed and bedded down, I grabbed a few hours of rest on the floor of the Kaltag community center. I woke up to television coverage of Martin Buser crossing the finish line in Nome. I must say that I felt a little jealous. I still had over 300 miles left to go. So I rousted up my team and headed out toward Unalakleet on the coast.

After traveling a few miles outside of town, all of a sudden the trees disappeared! I had reached the tundra line. This made me very uncomfortable. I was used to mushing on forest trails within the dense foliage of New England. Being out in the open made me feel cold and somewhat fearful. However, it didn't effect the dogs at all. I guess in their Siberian genetic memory the tundra is no big deal. After a while, I felt a little better, but I never really got used to the lack of trees.

At one point on that stretch, I found that I couldn't move my fingers. They were so cramped up from holding onto the sled that they were locked. Fortunately, my traveling buddy Jim Oehschlaeger happened along. He helped me fire up some hand warmers and change mittens. Believe me, it's a terrifying feeling when you can't work your zippers, particularly when it's time for a "pit stop." Thank heavens for Jim.

The trip to Unalakleet is about ninety miles, so most teams take a significant rest in between. A popular spot for stopping is called "Old Woman Cabin," a shack that sits right near the trail. It was there that I met Steve Fossett, a retired stockbroker from Chicago. Steve now spends his life moving from adventure to adventure. Having climbed many of the tallest mountains in the world, Steve had now set his sites on completing the Iditarod. To do this, he leased his team from one of the top Iditarod contenders in Alaska.

Steve's team was much faster than mine, but he was being extremely cautious in terms of his rest schedule. This strategy was successful since he went on to complete the race. In recent years, Steve Fossett has become famous as one of the leading contenders to be the first to sail a hot-air balloon around the world.

To the End of the Earth

When I got into Unalakleet, I was literally dog-tired. Earl had warned me that you become a zombie after awhile. I sure felt like one. I had to get some sleep. So after the dogs bedded down, so did I. I made my way to makeshift sleeping quarters that had been set up for mushers in the Unalakleet School. They had actually provided mattresses on the floor to sleep on. What luxury! I laid down my head and didn't wake up for six hours.

I guess I wasn't the only musher who needed sleep. As I was entering the school, I ran into Raymie Redington, who was leaving. Raymie was traveling with his father, Joe Redington, the father of the Iditarod. Raymie and I had chatted on and off throughout the race, and I always looked forward to his great sense of humor. Joe Sr. had run into trouble losing his team in the early part of the race. Raymie decided to stay with his dad for the remainder of the race to make sure he'd be okay.

From dawn 'til dusk. (Joe Asarisi)

"Boy, your dad's team looks good. They went by me like a freight train back there." I said to Raymie. "Yea, they're good when they're going. But they're never going. The old man sleeps way too much. We just spent several hours here. I got to get him moving." Out the door they went.

But I guess they didn't have enough sleep yet. After my extended six-hour nap, I made my way back to the dog lot. There I found Raymie and Joe lying on the ground next to their teams. They were both fast asleep. Of course, it didn't take very long at all for them to pass me again after I left the checkpoint.

From Unalakleet, the race trail winds its way through the Strawberry Hills to the remote village of Shaktoolik. Shaktoolik is a small fishing village that sits on a tiny spit of land jutting into Norton Sound on the Bering Sea. Earl called this place "the end of the earth," and I could see why. It is notorious for having some of the worst weather in the entire race. The wind is always blowing fiercely and there are no trees for protection.

The weather was absolutely silent when I pulled into the checkpoint. Fellow musher Kim Teasley told me "I've never seen it like this. This place is always blowing." We looked at each other. She was the first to say, "We better get going. It can't last." So we cut our rest period short, and headed out onto the trail. Before leaving, I dropped off my package of letters from Webster school children. This started an extended pen pal relationship between New Hampshire and Shaktoolik kids that lasted for the rest of the school year.

The stretch between Shaktoolik and Koyuk is potentially one of the most dangerous parts of the Iditarod Trail. Here the teams cross the frozen sea ice of Norton Sound. In bad weather, the trail becomes invisible. It would be easy for a musher to accidentally head out toward sea, where he or she could fall into open water. Sections of sea ice have also been known to drift away, stranding whoever is on board. Luck was with me that day, and I crossed with relative ease. Kim was already in the checkpoint when I arrived, as were several others.

Excitement in Koyuk

The Koyuk checkpoint was a small two-room building. Half of the facility was an open floor where mushers could sleep. The other half was set up with cots and a small kitchen for the veterinary staff to use. I had just lain down to sleep for a few minutes, when someone yelled "FIRE!"

One of the cookstoves in the veterinarians' section was burning out of control. The whole building could have easily gone up in flames. The weary mushers calmly (everyone was too tired to be excited) pulled together their outerwear and headed outside with the dog teams. A few minutes later, one of the vets popped his head out and said, "Everything's okay. You can come back in."

A few hours later, when it was time to leave, I mentioned to Kim: "Boy, we were lucky that the fire didn't get out of control." "What fire?" said Kim. I guess I had been too tired to be chivalrous. I didn't notice that Kim didn't evacuate with the rest of us. She had slept right through the fire. To this day, I don't think Kim believes that there ever was a fire! She thinks I was just kidding.

Before I was ready to leave, a trail official came into the checkpoint and told everyone that there was severe overflow on the way to Elim. It was going to be necessary to detour the trail to get around a particularly bad section. This made me nervous. I was still uncomfortable about traveling through this treeless section of Alaska and I was worried about getting lost. Kim, who was ready to go herself, offered to travel with me. She had trained many times in this area and was familiar with the landscape.

I was very grateful for this act of kindness. Kim had a much faster team than mine and it was obvious that I would only slow her down. The only reason she wasn't way ahead is that she had been nursing two very sick dogs back to health. She cared so much for her animals that she couldn't bring herself to drop these dogs when they got sick. She didn't think anyone would care for them

the way she did. By now, her team was healthy and she was starting to move up. Her offer to help me demonstrates the kind of sportsmanship and selflessness that the Iditarod stands for.

Elim and Mr. Science

The trip with Kim to Elim turned out to be one of my favorite days of the race. The sun was bright and clear and the view of Norton Sound was magnificent. The detour turned out to be no problem at all. We stopped a few times to snack the dogs, trade food between ourselves, and enjoy the beautiful scenery. All the dogs were healthy and things were really looking good for a strong finish in the next few days.

Just before we got to Elim, the trail dropped down out of the hills onto the frozen ice of Norton Sound. As we approached the village, I saw two young Eskimo children fishing in an open lead near the shore. We passed by a beautiful old fishing boat that had been put up for winter. You couldn't paint a prettier postcard of Alaska than what I saw that day.

Elim embraces the Iditarod and the mushers that make it to their tiny village. Near the checkpoint, a young Eskimo boy, probably no more than 5 years old, came to gawk at my dogs. I picked him up, put him on the sled, and gave him a ride to the stopping point. I'll never forget the look of delight on his face. Later, an elder villager came to chat with me about sled dogs and life in Alaska. There is a gentleness and kindness in the Eskimo people that is hard to describe. You can see it in their manner and hear it in their voices. I feel privileged to have met so many of these wonderful people as a result of my mushing experience.

The checkpoint itself was in a newly built community center in the heart of town. There I again met up with many of my traveling buddies, including Jim Oehschlaeger and Steve Christon. It is common wisdom that a musher shouldn't spend too much time in this checkpoint. You are getting close to the end of the race. White Mountain, where you are required to take a mandatory eight-hour rest, is less than fifty miles away. To be really competitive, you should probably move through Elim as quickly as possible. Our group, however, wasn't going to bypass the hospitality of this wonderful town. Even though temperatures were well below zero, Elim was the warmest place on the trail.

Jim Oehschlaeger was sponsored by the manufacturers of MREs, *Meals Ready to Eat,* a portable military ration. These ingenious kits have a built-in chemical heater. You just add a little water, and within seconds you get a steaming hot meal. (I can't vouch for the taste.) Jim (a.k.a. Mr. Science) decided to demonstrate this remarkable process to a group of excited Eskimo kids in the Community Center. The kids squealed and laughed as much as they would have for any Las Vegas magic show.

Our spirits were high, but we eventually had to leave Elim. It was getting pretty dark as I pulled up a fairly steep mountainside just beyond the village. All of the sudden, the team began to bunch up. I couldn't really see what was happening as I called out to the leaders to move forward.

They gradually moved ahead, but then it happened again. What was going on? I planted the snow hook and walked up to the front to see two of the dogs tied together. I had been struggling for the last few days to arrange the dogs in my team to avoid accidental breedings. Two of the bitches had come into season, including Taiga, the one dog on the team that Donna and I owned. Taiga was being bred by Curley, the number one lead dog on the team. Even though they were tied, they still tried to keep running. What sled dogs! Eventually, Taiga gave birth to several puppies, some of which are running on my current team.

On to Nome

Mushers are required to rest at least eight hours in the final wilderness checkpoint of White Mountain. From there, it is less than 100 miles to the finish line. I pulled into the village just as a windstorm was kicking up. My dogs ate and rested well. So I managed to get about four hours of sleep. We were all ready to go at the end of this mandatory layover.

The weather between White Mountain and the finish line is notorious. Frequent windstorms make it impossible to stay on the trail. Mushers and their teams pass over seven peaks through the Topcok Hills before they drop down onto the coast for the last fifty or so miles into Nome. Fortunately, the wind was mild as I went over these mountains in relative ease. This was all about to change when I reached the coast.

As soon as I got out of the mountains, I was greeted by a wall of wind and blowing snow. It was still daylight, but I could just barely make out the trail. The way was marked with large tripods that were strategically placed every few hundred yards. I was nervous, but my lead dog Curley was not. Perhaps he felt particularly confident because he had recently mated Taiga. Perhaps he still remembered the way from his previous trip to Nome in the 1990 Iditarod. Whatever the reason, Curley pushed forward through the drifting snow.

Just as the weather was really getting bad, Jim Oehschlaeger came up from behind me. He appeared out of nowhere like a white knight on a horse. His team seemed to float through the air, since the wind was so bad that you couldn't see the ground. A few miles later, we passed through to the other side of the storm. The weather was suddenly very calm. Shortly thereafter, Jim and I were joined by Cliff Robertson, another first-time Iditarod racer. The three of us arrived together in Safety, the last checkpoint before the finish line. We now only had about twenty miles to go before we reached Nome.

A reporter from the Nome radio station interviewed me as soon as I arrived. "Do you have any messages to pass on to the folks waiting at the finish line?" she asked. I said: "Please tell the mayor that I have a message from the Governor of New Hampshire to the people of Nome. It's sort of a greeting from one of the oldest states to one of the newest." I also knew that Donna would be waiting for me at the finish line. In keeping with our plan, she had flown in a few days earlier. "Tell my wife that I love her and that the dogs and I miss her" I added. "We look forward to seeing you in Nome." Off I went.

After leaving the checkpoint, I put on a portable radio headset to listen to the race coverage of the people finishing ahead of me. Jim and Cliff were traveling a little faster than me and pulled ahead. I doubted that I would see them again before the finish line. As I listened to the radio, an announcement was made that a generous benefactor had donated an all expenses paid trip to Hawaii for the fiftieth place finisher. I knew from the race coverage that the fiftieth finisher would be Jim, Cliff, or me. I also knew that I was the only one with a radio. The other guys didn't know about the prize.

About five miles outside of town I came upon Cliff, who was dealing with a massive tangle. I told him about the contest. "I was robbed," he said, "I was robbed!" Apparently, Cliff had some bitches in season on his team. Jim had come up next to him and the two teams had gotten tangled. Inadvertently, two of Cliff's dogs had tied. Jim went on while Cliff had to wait for his dogs to finish. As it turns out, the prize for fiftieth was a hoax anyway. But at least temporarily, it added a little excitement to the finish.

I had very mixed feelings as I came within sight of Nome. At this point, I knew that I would finish the race successfully. I felt very proud of my dogs and myself. This was an accomplishment of a lifetime. I also looked forward to a hot shower and a warm bed. Most of all, I really looked forward to seeing Donna.

I also felt very sad that my great adventure was drawing to a close. I had planned and prepared for this race for nearly two years. Now it was just about over. Soon, I would be flying back to my beloved New Hampshire and resuming a normal

The finish line. (Joe Asarisi)

working schedule. My life as a full-time dog musher was ending.

I entered the final stretch of road to the famed burled arches in Nome. As I pulled the New Hampshire flag out of my sled, I was greeted by a police car, who set off his siren and flashing lights. The town's civil defense alarm went off to announce that another Iditarod musher was about to finish. It was Saturday night and the people poured out of bars to greet me. Donna was there to hug me, as was the mayor of Nome. I was also greeted by several of the mushers that had finished ahead of me, including Kim Teasley and Jim Oehschlaeger. Martin Buser, the race winner, shook my hand as I crossed the finish line. Martin, ever the gracious winner, stayed in Nome to greet all of the finishers that year.

As it turns out, I was very fortunate to finish when I did. Steve Christon finished several hours later. Then nobody finished for two more days. Several mushers had been unable to make their way through the coastal storm and had to camp in their sleds on the trail until the weather cleared. One musher, Bob Ernisse, had frozen his hands in the storm and had to be rescued only twenty-five miles from the finish. Imagine, having to scratch when you're that close to the finish! Fortunately, Bob was not discouraged and went on to complete the race in 1994.

Earl caught up with us a few days later in Nome. He was on his way to serve as race marshal in the Hope race, a 1,000-mile event that went from Nome to Siberia. Earl congratulated the dogs and me. Yet another team from the Howling Dog Farm had made its way across Alaska to successfully complete the Iditarod. We had proven once again that Siberian Huskies still have the right stuff.

Postscript

Donna and I stayed in Nome for several days and enjoyed the hospitality of the community. However, spring was rapidly approaching and we soon made our way back east with very fond

Earl Norris and Pete Johnson standing under the official finish line after Pete finished the Iditarod. (Donna Johnson)

memories of our great adventure in Alaska. We both had tears in our eyes when our plane landed in Boston. Alaska was magnificent, but there's nothing like coming home to New England. When we crossed the border into New Hampshire, we pulled our truck over and stopped to kiss the ground. We were home again.

Since 1992, Donna and I have continued to run cross-country races (60 to 250 miles) in New England and Canada. We also now enjoy winter camping by dog team. Our kennel has grown significantly since I ran the Iditarod. And we still stick with Siberian Huskies, the breed that we love and trust when we make our way out into the wilderness.

Many people ask me if I'm going to run the race again. I feel the same way now that I did when I crossed the finish line. If I ever get the opportunity, I'll jump at the chance to run the Iditarod again. Of course, I'll only do it under one condition. I need to have the right kind of dogs—Siberian Huskies.

(Winter Churchill Photography)

CHAPTER 12

What You Should Know About Breeding

It's expensive, it's time- and energy-consuming, and the frustrations almost always outnumber the successes: Those are the cold, hard facts of dog breeding. At its very best, it is only a partially self-sustaining hobby and should never be approached even as a break-even proposition, much less a potential profit-turning business. The costs of conscientious dog maintenance are just too high: hip x-rays, yearly eye exams, inoculations, dog food, kennel construction and maintenance, assorted supplies and tools, and sometimes thousands of dollars in crisis veterinary care, to name just a few of the obvious expenses. And those costs probably double with even modest participation in the dog show game; and without that participation or its equivalent in the working side of the breed, where does the potential breeder learn what a truly good Siberian is?

So the most important part in the art of dog breeding is the art of balancing it with the rest of your life, as part of a balanced ecosystem, and not to let it become a compulsive disorder that overwhelms everything else, particularly your bank account. Go slow, have fun, learn as you go, and understand it as a very long-term hobby whose real reward is in the day-to-day interaction with wonderful animals and not in the occasional rush of a blue ribbon, or a blue-and-white ribbon, or even a purple-and-gold ribbon (though those moments of recognition can be very validating).

It is a long, hard process to breed good dogs, involving lots of trial and error, an enormous amount of self-education, and, eventually, a little good luck. It requires great patience and determination, as does any art form, and certainly dog breeding is more of an art than it is anything else.

Nap time in the whelping box for eight grays and a red.

THE ART OF BREEDING: DEVELOPING AN EYE

In fact, in his book, *The New Art of Breeding Better Dogs,* Kyle Onstott makes the point that breeding is an art, not a science; by which I think he means, not only is the manipulation of seventy-eight chromosomes too vast and unpredictable an undertaking to manage on a purely scientific basis, but even more important, breeding is first and foremost about "seeing."

The dam of a litter normally begins to lose her coat a few weeks after her puppies are born.

A Siberian breeder is an artist who creates living artworks according to his or her observations of two dogs (and their pedigrees) and their relative relationship to the written Standard of the breed and to an idealized animal running around somewhere inside his or her head. So the first, and ever-ongoing job of would-be breeders is to train their eyes and imaginations toward their ideal, an ideal that should be based on historical, functional, and aesthetic perspectives, as well as the precise details of the written Standard, which is itself based on those perspectives.

Historical Viewpoint

The breed we know as the Siberian Husky came to the North American continent as an extremely sweet-tempered, foxy-looking (if somewhat varied), not very large working dog who could simply outrun anything on four legs that would pull a sled for long miles in arctic conditions.

Functional Viewpoint

In order to do this, we know—both from pictorial evidence, observer testimony, and what contemporary research on the working dog has shown to be necessarily true—that he had to have good feet, longer leg length than chest depth, a long upper arm, a double coat, a body only slightly longer than tall, intelligence, and heart (something which the great dog driver "Doc" Lombard once said is spelled GUTS).

Aesthetic Viewpoint

If dog shows are not merely fashion shows, where the overall look of a breed is allowed to change according to the whim of the day, then aesthetic ideals must be based historically and functionally. The early Siberians were certainly a varied lot, and perhaps their paint jobs (color and markings) were not so fancy as those of contemporary show dogs. They were, however, consistently quite foxy-looking and built efficiently for their task. From these early dogs were gleaned the ideals of type—ear shape and size, skull shape, eye set, coat type, body proportions, tail set and carriage, and more—that paved the way for the Siberian Husky as we know it.

There is always going to be a range of what is acceptable, in terms of the Standard, and a narrower range of what is excellent, but unless a breeder can appraise a Siberian from these various viewpoints, only dumb luck will let him or her produce a truly good one.

BE WILLING TO LEARN, SLOWLY

Of course, every Siberian is a little different, none is perfect, and even more problematical, every judge and every breeder sees every dog just a little differently. So learning to see requires a great deal of looking and listening. It takes years, and usually involves numerous revisions and corrections of ones original impressions and ideals. It should also involve learning from a number of different mentors—show breeders, racers, judges, authors and even sometimes people far outside the Siberian fold—sighthound people, for instance, or field trial enthusiasts.

It is important therefore, not to be too hasty. A sad fact of the dog game is that most fanciers participate only about five years—because they make mistakes, or have bad luck and get discouraged. And the most frequent mistake is simply acquiring too many animals too quickly, overburdening their resources of time, money, and space, as well as making future developments too dependent on selecting animals before developing a truly educated, judicious "eye."

In short, if every would be breeder spent several years acquiring both a hands on "feel" and more abstract knowledge of its history, function and aesthetic ideals, we'd have many fewer mediocre specimens of the Siberian and many fewer frustrated people.

AIM FOR GOOD DOGS, NOT JUST WINNERS

The goal of every wise breeder is to produce a consistent level of good, sound, happy, healthy, typey puppies most of whom will be sold as pets. Temperament, then, must remain at all times a primary issue, along with type and basic athleticism. Compromising temperament is the most dangerous thing a breeder can do because it produces unwanted animals, perhaps hurting the breeder's reputation and certainly hurting the breed's.

Outgrowing the whelping box.

This is not to say, however, that all Siberian puppies should exhibit a gundog unflappability in the face of every strange and/or noisy circumstance. A certain skittishness is quite common among younger animals at various stages of development, particularly bitches in adolescence. Usually they outgrow it, but if you wish, for example, to show a given puppy, it should be socialized with a certain caution in the full recognition of what weird places dog shows really are from a dog's point of view: hundreds of dog noises and smells, loudspeakers, and, particularly indoors, a noise level that can only be described as an unholy din amid lurid, noxious clouds of chalk, dust, and hairspray, swirled this way and that by dragon-necked, roaring hair dryers.

So the wise breeder does not aim for the quickest way into the ribbons if it means compromising on temperament, type, or health. He or she knows that so-called great dogs simply happen (1 in 400 says Earl Norris) and sometimes they happen after years of hard work, and sometimes they happen out of dumb luck.

But a top-winning animal that comes from a long line of happy, healthy, typey, athletic animals is much more likely to be of service to the breed than the big winner whose mother lacked type, whose father was epileptic, and whose grandmother cowered under her dog house for most of her life. The former may be truly a great dog, the latter simply a big winner who is likely to do more harm than good to the breed.

SELECTING STOCK

Once you've started developing an ideal, an eye, select breeding stock on the basis of their

Everyone wants a piece of the pie. (Cheryl Scheall)

approximation to this ideal. Get lots of advice, sift it, and adopt what makes sense. It usually pays, for instance, to bring along two family strains simultaneously, along with some sort of outcross potential. Study pedigrees, but don't become obsessed with them. Too many inferior animals are bred by people in love with what the pedigree looks like, and not enough on what the actual animals look like. Know what lines produce what characteristics (both good and bad) on a fairly regular basis. Realize every individual varies enough that the issue on any given breeding should be the actual dogs themselves, their phenotypes, and only secondarily their pedigrees. As much as possible, breed like to like in terms of the strengths of the pair, and unlike to unlike in terms of faults. That is to say double up on

Several colors will often be included in the same Siberian litter: here a black, a gray, and a white. A well-bred litter will reflect consistency throughout.

The so-called "red" color phase depends on a simple recessive gene, so reds bred to reds will produce only reds.

strengths and don't double up on weaknesses.

TYPES OF BREEDING

Generally speaking, there are three kind of breeding: linebreeding (though purists in the field of genetics dislike the term), inbreeding, and outcrossing.

So-called line breeding—that is matings between dogs that are loosely related within three or four generations—has long been the staple of consistent, fairly safe breeding practices in both contemporary and primitive cultures. Inbreeding—the breeding of cousins and closer relatives—can yield dramatic, sometimes lovely, sometimes disastrous results, and should only be undertaken with great caution and probably some years of experience. Outcrossing—the breeding of unrelated animals—is only partially possible in a breed as generally related as the Siberian. The best use of outcrossing is as an occasional way to avoid painting yourself into a corner—to bring in new and (hopefully) desirable characteristics and to refresh the gene pool from time to time. It's less predictable than either linebreeding or inbreeding, but an integral part of any long-range breeding program. It should be understood that, in fact, we are always reinventing the breed with each generation, and that genetic variety is important for maintaining both vigor and type.

The burden of motherhood often includes factors of inheritance. It is obvious that these puppies' father did not carry the red gene.

ASSESSING AND APPRAISING, AN ONGOING PRACTICE

Once you have acquired a promising animal or two, start assessing them and your early breeding results. Some lines may work for you better than others, but remember—just as there are no perfect specimens, there are no perfect lines. Every breeding is a gambling game played with seventy-eight chromosomes and is, therefore, something of a "crapshoot." So don't blame everything on the original breeder when things go wrong. If it were easy, we'd all have perfect dogs and there would be no reason for dog shows, dog races, or any other arena in which we measure our dogs' comparative merit.

Study the growth patterns in your puppies and the ongoing development in your adults. Different lines develop at different rates, and understanding the differences will affect your selection of which dogs you will keep. Many breeders will assess overall balance sometime in the first few days of the puppies' lives, before they develop enough body fat to obscure the outline of the skeleton. Type manifests itself in puppies at 4 or 5 weeks when the ears come up (if they come up at that age) and are still relatively small. But movement is very clumsy and cannot be assessed with any reasonable degree of accuracy until puppies reach 7 or 8 weeks. Sometime between 6 and 9 weeks, puppies theoretically pass through phases of miniature adulthood before getting down to the serious job of growing.

As they grow, many puppies go through awkward stages in which their heads may appear small or narrow in relation to their overall body proportions. They may be narrow in front or high behind, long-tailed, or just plain gawky. Some take on that gawky look by 10 or 11 weeks and don't

Some shades of gray begin with considerable buff coloring, especially on the head. (Sue Shane)

look good again until they are 2 or 3 years old. Most will have periodic foreshadowings of promising adulthood—often 6 to 9 months is particularly appealing. But even those puppies who always seem to grow in proportion to themselves often go through a gawky adolescence as the beautiful puppy seems to vanish with the first shed of coat, leaving something behind that is suddenly unrecognizable—scrawny, hairless, big-eared, and narrow-headed. Most, however, do make the return from the *land of the uglies!*

In looking at puppies, don't make the common mistake of falling in love with the biggest male in every litter, or the blackest coat, or the blue-eyed ones. Look deeper. Look for balance, agility, type, and temperament. Think first in terms of the whelping box, second in terms of the show ring.

Select animals on the basis of their positive characteristics, not just the absence of obvious faults. The slightly narrow-in-the-rear animal with the great front may be more valuable to you than the better-in-the-rear but not-so-good-in-front, flashier animal. Peggy Koehler of Alakazan Kennels once remarked that the art of picking puppies involved the ability to pick the *best puppy in a litter, not the best puppy in the world*. Moreover, different sorts of puppies may be valuable at different points in a breeding program—depending on which battles have been won and lost.

Don't fall into the "teddy bear" or "big bear" syndromes of either selecting only the cute stubby animals or the big-chested, heavy-boned monsters. Look for the moderate, the athletic, and where possible, the slow to mature. Broad heads usually prefigure broad chests; long heads generally go with long backs and loss of breed type; short necks often mean steep shoulders; while loose skin usually indicates loose tendons and muscles. As important as the proper length and angle of each bone in the skeleton is, it is not nearly so crucial to the health and performance of an animal as the soft tissue—heart, lungs, muscles, tendons, ligaments.

It's generally best to avoid breeding extremes, a very large dog to a very small bitch, for instance, because often the resulting litter will simply split into big ones and little ones, rather than providing a blend.

In most litters, you can generally identify at least one puppy that resembles each parent, and often individuals that resemble each grandparent; so grandparents are extremely important in the consideration of any breeding. Furthermore, if the imagined blend of two animals does not actually turn up in a given breeding, be patient; it may well turn up in the next generation.

RATING YOUR DOGS

Once you own a breeding nucleus of a few dogs and have an ideal in mind, it's a great help to establish some sort of rating system on a scale of 1 to 10, for instance. The 10 would be perfect (and therefore impossible to achieve), with the minimum for a championship-caliber Siberian being perhaps a 6. Each factor you'd like to change in your animal gets a unit of 1 subtracted from the ideal 10. (Some factors, of course, might get more heavily weighted, as in the case of temperament problems or entirely faulty portions of the assembly, or bad coat or poor type.) Animals critically appraised at, say, 7s and 8s are really very good dogs; if bred judiciously, with few common obvious or latent fault-tendencies and sufficient common strengths and similarities, the resulting litter could include some truly excellent individuals.

An even more thorough rating system can be established by instituting the 1 to 10 scale in several categories: type, temperament, athleticism and overall balance and movement. In such a system, of course 10s *are* possible, and ratings where the sum totals of the parents are 16 or better in each category are certainly breedings worth trying—unless their pedigrees indicate a doubling up on potential health problems.

Consistency is reflected in the offspring of the winners of the Stud Dog class, the Brood Bitch class, and the Best of Breed winner, herself, at the 1998 National Specialty under judge Merc Cresap. (Jean Edwards)

Thus a dog rated a 7 for type (a bit short-coated and plain in head), a 10 for temperament, an 8 for athleticism (quick and well-muscled but a little steep in shoulder), and a 6 for overall balance and movement (a little short on extension) might be an excellent match for a bitch rated a 9 for type (ears well-set but a bit tall, wonderful head and coat), a 7 for temperament (friendly, workable but a little wary of strange circumstances), and a 9 for balance and movement.

The method is really not that important. The point is to keep the quality of your animals high in as many categories as possible, and your litters as consistent as possible, while avoiding all the hidden

With a view toward tomorrow—puppy panache. (Sue Shane)

At 9 to 12 weeks, puppies' ears begin to grow before their heads do. (Winter Churchill Photography)

A little shade, a newly dug, cool hole: Life's good. Spacious, comfortable, secure facilities are essential to a smooth kennel operation.

Talking it over with Mom, whose laid-back ears indicate the degree of her devotion. (Sue Shane)

health problems that inevitably plague any breed, especially one as popular and numerous as the Siberian Husky.

Wise breeders breed for themselves, not for what the judges want, even though a nice win puts a nice spin on a dog show day.

Similarly, the wise breeder does not make supplying dogs that appeal to current fashion a priority. In the show ring, there will always be inevitable swings of the pendulum of fashion and focus—large

Type and consistency . . . in spades! (The dog is on the left, the bitch is on the right.)

Mom, daughter, and grandson: three generations of smiling faces and excellent type. (Jean Edwards)

admiration for size and bulk as a first aesthetic principle. Anyone who has ever walked through a densely populated area with a Siberian Husky will have met incredible numbers of people whose brother or cousin or friend owns "one of those Huskies who's *this* tall." In the telling, the teller's eyes grow larger as he floridly describes this veritable mountain of canine splendor.

Last, but certainly not least, wise breeders progress only at the rate their resources of time, money, and energy allow. They know their most valuable kennel run is the empty one waiting to house the next promising puppy. They know that over the course of time the small kennel can contribute as much to the breed as the large kennel, that in fact the well-managed small kennel is usually more efficient than its larger counterpart, and a lot more fun. And they always remember that their particular art form lives, breathes, and is meant to share pleasure, that every dog in their yard deserves their love, respect, and attention.

to small, red to gray, one marking pattern to another. The possibilities are endless.

In the pet world beyond the disciplines of the show ring, there is the simple, if uninformed,

CHAPTER 13

Our Gentle Geriatrics

BY JEAN FOURNIER

In general, Siberian Huskies are blessed with quite long lives, frequently 15 to 18 years, though they are vulnerable to cancer and other diseases of aging from 8 to 10 years. Your daily interactions with your dog offer the best opportunity to notice early signs of that inevitable aging. Vomiting, diarrhea, a change in eating habits, increased drinking or urination, sudden weight gain or loss, or decreased activity can signal age-related illnesses such as kidney disease, Cushing's disease, heart disease, or dental problems. Many of these ailments can be greatly alleviated with early detection, which is why annual or semiannual veterinary checkups, along with a blood and urine analysis, are critical. Research indicates that dogs are living longer than ever, thanks in part to the efforts of research conducted at veterinary colleges, food and drug companies, and animal behaviorists, and early detection of an array of age-related problems can add years to your dog's life.

ARTHRITIS

This crippling disease systematically damages the joints of more than 8 million dogs every year. It typically starts with injury to the joint cartilage, resulting from trauma, genetic predisposition, or simply old age. It dramatically affects a dog's mobility and activity level, and can hamper such simple, routine activities as rising from a sitting position or negotiating stairs. Symptoms typically occur from about 11 years old, but in Siberians these may not show up until the dog is considerably older. Fortunately, there are many excellent medications that combat arthritis and arthritis pain, many of which are quite new, and your vet can advise you about which is most appropriate to the condition of your Siberian.

NUTRITION

Young Siberians, especially those regularly involved in strenuous physical activities, typically thrive on very high energy foods often designed specifically for working dogs. However, as dogs age, it is important to modify the diet by reducing quantity and protein levels, perhaps adding vitamins and lowering calcium and phosphorous intake. Many owners overfeed even their younger animals because the dramatic, yearly shedding process can make the out-of-coat Siberian Husky appear starkly gaunt and emaciated. However, a fat young dog is more likely to become a fat old dog when the impact of poor condition on health poses an even greater danger to the dog's overall well-being.

OBESITY

Obesity is the most common nutritional disorder in dogs. By some estimates, at least a quarter of all dogs weigh more than 20 percent over their optimal weight, and a large number of these portly dogs are seniors. Obese Siberians have greater incidence of skin disease, diabetes, kidney failure, heart problems, and other maladies. Since fat cells require oxygen, an overweight dog's heart and lungs work harder to meet that demand. Excess pounds also put additional stress on skeletal joints, thereby aggravating early onset of arthritis. Furthermore, being overweight has a negative effect on fertility; males often experience lowered sperm count, and overweight females are at increased risk of complications during pregnancy and labor. Owners should carefully monitor their dog's weight on scales at home or at their vet's, as well as making a periodic assessment by "feel." By stroking your dog's sides, you should be able to easily feel, but not see, his ribs. And viewing from above, you should be able to easily determine that your Siberian's waist is noticeably narrower than his rib cage.

Obesity does not occur overnight. It evolves from an imbalance of excercise and caloric intake, often in the form of too many treats and an overabundance of easy living. Substituting carrots or celery for other treats can have a dramatic effect on a reemerging waistline, as can supplementing meals with canned unsalted green beans and a regular regimen of daily walks on lead. And while it is difficult to resist that pitiful look in the skillful beggar's eyes when you are eating and he's not, simply remind yourself that you may be adding years to your Siberian's life simply by resisting that mournful gaze. Moreover, in time, a Siberian usually becomes accustomed to the new regimen.

AGING EYES

Your Siberian's eloquent eyes are one of his most endearing features. They are also complex sensory organs that help him navigate his world.

Petroushka Rourlin as an energetic yearling (left) and as a dignified 9-year-old (right).

Occasionally, owners confuse the cloudiness of thickening lenses, common to old age, with old-age cataracts, and since the Siberian breed is often affected by a number of eye anomalies, some danger signs should be noted. Eye conditions characterized by redness, discharge, squinting, or sudden vision loss are quite obvious and may be signs of serious afflictions. Glaucoma, progressive retinal atrophy, and other ailments may appear in the older dog and can be treated in a number of ways. Many other problems can also be avoided by adhering to the following rules:

Regal repose: Ch. Demavand's Shiva at 10 years old. (JoLynn Stresing)

- Keep chemicals (even shampoos) away from your dog's eyes.

- Keep your dog's head INSIDE moving vehicles.

- Carefully control a diabetic dog's blood sugar.

- Schedule regular eye exams for the older Siberian.

- Before adopting or rescuing a Siberian, make sure to have its eyes examined and cleared by a board-certified ophthalmologist who was referred by your vet.

- Don't breed from or to dogs that are known carriers of genes for eye diseases. Much progress is presently being made to determine carriers of eye abnormalities in Siberians through the AKC Canine Health Research Foundation project.

Your Siberian's elderly eyes are windows to the inner world that not only reveal his soul but also his general health. The eyes of a dog in good health are clear, free of discharge, and lively enough for the dog to convince his owner that he still "knows best."

A VACCINATION PLAN AND REGULAR VETERINARY VISITS

It is extremely important to maintain a vaccination schedule, even in older dogs. Vaccine-produced immunity lasts only about a year and is not "built up" over time. And even if you administer your own vaccines, though not entirely recommended, it is important to maintain annual or biannual veterinary checkups for the older dog to detect heart murmurs, periodontal disease, suspicious lumps and bumps, kidney or liver disease, and a multitude of other existing ailments.

BEHAVIOR AS A SYMPTOM

The most common behavior-altering diseases among older dogs are arthritis and dental disease, but decreased vision and hearing may also impact on a senior's normal behavior patterns. The following checklist, however, is intended to alert the owner to behavior that should be brought to the attention of your veterinarian:

- Wanders aimlessly and appears lost or confused

- Gets "stuck" in corners, under or behind furniture

Creature comforts.

- Stares into space or at walls
- Has difficulty finding the door
- Does not recognize familiar people
- Does not respond to verbal cues or his name
- Solicits attention less than before
- Less likely to stand for petting or walks away
- Sleeps more in a 24-hour period
- Sleeps less at night
- Urinates or defecates indoors and was always house trained
- Forgets the reason for going outdoors
- Exhibits separation anxiety
- Exhibits noise phobias
- Exhibits signs of depression or mourning
- Exhibits inter-dog aggression and dominance
- Excessive vocalization, often for no apparent reason

Any of these symptoms may indicate disorders that are often treatable and can improve the quality of life for your dog and the quality of his relationship with you and other family members.

WHEN IT'S TIME TO SAY GOOD-BYE

Someone once said, it's not that dogs have feelings; they ARE feelings. Their joys and griefs are palpable in their body language and being. So when a much-loved old dog reaches the point in a prolonged illness where he cannot be helped by veterinary medicine or our very best care and attention, it's time to make that hardest of all decisions. Any caring owner must know whether to authorize euthanasia and when to do so. Often, it can be hard not to be selfish and prolong life no matter what because we can't bear the departure of such a faithful companion. But there comes a time in many dogs' lives when that choice is the only kindness we have left to offer. It's a decision and process that should normally involve the entire family. Many of us choose to spend the final moments with our friend, stroking his head and speaking gently as he drifts painlessly off. It is comforting to us to know that the last voice and touch he remembers is ours.

ON COPING WITH PET LOSS

The substantial grief we feel at the loss of a devoted pet is often hard for friends and family to understand, but all real "dog people" understand perfectly. It is an enormous loss from our lives. If you feel you lack support during such a time, ask your veterinarian for the name or number of a nearby college that has social workers specifically trained to counsel pet owners. Another way to soften the loss is to make a donation in your pet's name to a worthy animal-related cause. Humane organizations need financial support to care for homeless pets, and many veterinary and dog-related organizations accept scholarships and funds in the donor's name in honor of your loss.

On the passing of a Siberian friend at age 16, the following thoughts were shared during that almost unbearable grieving period:

In the weeks since his death, I have found myself thinking about the unique feelings many of us have for our dogs. Perhaps it is irrational to heap so much affection on an animal when human beings are so distressed throughout the world, and maybe we do it because, like young children, they are totally dependent on us.

But unlike children, who individually reach beyond, our pets are forever bound to us by an indestructible bond of faith and comradeship. For them, there is no other world except the one we create . . . and in that there is an intoxicating security for both.

So enjoy to the fullest your beautiful, cheerful Siberian during all the days of his life and continue to appreciate his worth and cherish his indelible memory after he is gone.

CHAPTER 14

The Siberian Husky Club of America, Inc.

BY DONNA BECKMAN, PRESIDENT, AND DELBERT L. THACKER, SECRETARY

"In August 1930, the American Kennel Club asked my husband to prepare a Standard for the Siberian Husky, looking forward to a possible recognition of the breed. Recognition was given in October, and at this time thoroughbred Siberian Huskies are eligible to registration."

The quote from the foregoing article was the first written for the *AKC Gazette* by Fay Clark Hurley of Fairbanks, Alaska, that outlined many historical events leading up to the development of the present-day Siberian Husky Club of America (SHCA). Contained within the Archives of the Siberian Husky Club of America are precious documents that illustrate the metamorphosis of our beloved breed, its Standard, and the development of the parent club.

The first Standard for the Siberian Husky, appears in the April 1, 1932, issue of *Pure-Bred Dogs— American Kennel Gazette*. The article entitled, "New Standards Approved," states, "Since the publication of *Pure-Bred Dogs,* two new breeds, the Keeshond and the Siberian Husky, have been added to the list of breeds recognized by the American Kennel Club. While no breed club for either has been formed in the

United States, the American Kennel Club is publishing herewith a Standard of perfection of these two breeds."

Contained in other volumes of the Siberian Husky Archives, are letters dating back to 1937, which deal with various meetings, letters, and reports relating to the formation of the breed club. Several articles are worth mentioning. In a document dated October 21, 1937, names were listed as the organizing Siberian Club. Those individuals were Dean C. F. Jackson, Mr. and Mrs. Milton Seeley, Mrs. Jackson, Mrs. Samuel Post, and Miss Margaret Dewey. From this core group numerous letters were written, and by March of 1938 the first list of fanciers had been expanded to thirty-eight individuals/addresses. A letter from Charles Inglee, executive vice-president of the American Kennel Club (AKC), to Short Seeley, dated April 8, 1938, outlined the first steps directed by the AKC for the development of our breed club.

"Your letter of April 5 was received this morning, and I hasten to comply with your request for information relative to procedure in organizing your new Siberian Husky Club."

The letter continues to explain that a sample copy of a constitution and by-laws was included to assist with the development of an SHCA constitution. Upon completion, Mr. Inglee requested a copy of the final constitution and a list of officers/members, and he mentioned that the admission fee was $250 with annual fees of $10.

On April 19th, 1938, a meeting of interested individuals for the sole purpose of forming a breed club was held at the Middlesex Kennel Club dog show in Cambridge, Massachusetts. The following officers were elected:

President: Dean C. F. Jackson
Vice-President: Mrs. Samuel Post
Secretary/Treasurer: Mrs. Milton (Short) Seeley.

Additionally, an Advisory Committee consisting of Mrs. Kaare Nansen, Mr. Leonhard Seppala, Judge Coke Hill, Mr. Clarence Grey, and Mrs. Birdsall Darling was formed. After many letters to AKC, and hours of dedication by those previously mentioned, the Siberian Husky Club of America was formed. The pioneers of the breed weathered many trials and tribulations from 1930 to 1938 to create the SHCA.

Those first New Englanders began their association with the original Siberian Huskies brought to the region by Leonhard Seppala, a member of the Advisory Committee. These fanciers were initially mushers who established the rich sledding history in New England. These first enthusiasts so admired these small dogs from Siberia, they dedicated enormous effort in gaining recognition for the breed. They concentrated their efforts on behalf of the Siberian Husky through the formation of the Siberian Husky Club of America, and obtaining recognition of the Siberian Husky as a recognized purebred dog through opening the stud book with the American Kennel Club, the official registering body for the entire United States.

In the early days, SHCA had the flavor of a local breed club. Most of the founding fanciers were located in the states of New Hampshire and Massachusetts. The attorney who worked with the

Club on its incorporation was a fancier of another breed and a neighbor of Lorna Demidoff, one of the breed's most respected enthusiasts. (Even to this day, SHCA's legal firm remains the same, and the Club's attorney is the son of that original incorporation attorney.)

When it came time to incorporate, SHCA's meager treasury couldn't cover the incorporation fee. However, a young enthusiast by the name of Roland Lombard generously paid for SHCA to become *SHCA, Inc.* That man would later become a legend both in the Siberian Husky world and in the sport of sled dog racing. The long-standing rivalry between "Doc" Lombard and Alaskan George Attla was the stuff of which glorious legends are made.

From those early beginnings of SHCA, its role was clear: to follow the evolutionary path of the Siberian and to keep the best interest of this breed foremost in mind and deed.

Although many were initially interested in the Siberian as a working sled dog, fanciers soon wanted an off-season activity. Entries of Siberian Huskies in local dog shows began to grow. And, in response to this need, SHCA held its first Specialty show in 1940. Because of its need to serve its membership and the Siberian Husky community, the first several years of SHCA Specialties were held in New England, where the greatest population of fanciers lived.

World War II somewhat reduced the activity of SHCA and other dog clubs. During this time, some SHCA members turned their talents toward training dogs for the war effort. SHCA members and Siberian fanciers also participated in the training of sled teams for the expeditions that would be mounted.

The postwar days brought a boon to the popularity of the Siberian Husky. Siberians began appearing in locations outside New England. Soon Siberians were being bred, raced, and shown all across the United States. In lockstep with this migration, SHCA found itself really beginning to serve America. The Club responded with the *Newsletter,* through which its growing membership could keep in touch. Over the years the *Newsletter* has grown in popularity and content, and has twice won the award for Best National Club Publication from the Dog Writers Association of America.

The postwar popularization of the Siberian Husky prompted the Club to take on a more national quality, with increasing numbers of committee chairmen and members of the Board of Directors living outside New England. Additionally, SHCA began conducting shows outside of its original area, with the first Specialty held outside of New England taking place in the mid-1950s. Since this time, SHCA Specialties have rotated around the country to give all fanciers an opportunity to attend a national Specialty in their local area. Throughout this entire time span SHCA Specialties were conducted in conjunction with all-breed shows. All that changed in the early 1970s when SHCA began holding independent Specialties.

In response to the membership's interest in the multi-faceted Siberian, SHCA created the Working-Showing Trophy. This is still arguably the most highly cherished award available to SHCA members. Although it is only awarded when there is sufficient competition, this beautiful silver punch bowl is awarded to the member whose Siberians have excelled both in the show ring and on the trail. Many of the breed's most outstanding examples have won this highly coveted award.

With the health and well-being of the Siberian foremost in the concerns of SHCA, the Club was among the first breed clubs to establish a committee to report on hip dysplasia. Thanks to this early educational effort and the early adoption of routine x-raying by SHCA members, the Siberian Husky is among the breeds with the lowest incidence of hip dysplasia.

Based on need, the Hip Dysplasia Committee soon evolved to become SHCA's current Genetics Committee. As hereditary eye problems were discovered in the breed, SHCA, its members, and other Siberian fanciers were early sponsors of the initial studies conducted on cataracts and corneal dystrophy in the Siberian Husky. And more recently, SHCA and the Siberian community are significant donors to the Canine Health Fund's research for the benefit of Siberians.

The 1970s was a time of extraordinary population growth for the Siberian Husky. Numbers of dogs and litters produced skyrocketed this breed to a place among the top twenty in popularity in the United States. To this unprecedented popularity, SHCA responded with a "Protection, Not Promotion" stance. The Club stepped up its educational efforts to inform those who were drawn to the beauty of the Siberian Husky that this is not the breed for everyone. Both in humorous and more serious ways, SHCA produced realistic portrayals of the Siberian Husky as a somewhat unusual breed.

Also in response to this new-found popularity, SHCA produced educational materials about genetic problems in the breed. These materials, still in use today, help breeders and potential owners understand the nature of these genetic problems and what to do to try to avoid them. To focus further on producing healthy dogs and placing them in good homes, SHCA developed some guidelines for ethical conduct. These documents take the SHCA Code of Ethics and further explain it, outlining ethical behavior in breeding, offering a dog at stud, and placing puppies and adult dogs.

Additionally, to meet this need for education among a rapidly growing fancy, in the mid-1970s, SHCA instituted annual educational seminars held in conjunction with the national Specialty. Topics have included structure and movement, history of the breed, seizures, eye problems, conformation, and many other topics of interest to the fancy.

Because this is a working breed that excels in the sport of sled dog racing, SHCA filled the void in the recognition of Siberians working on the trail. The Sled Dog Degree program provides Siberian fanciers with a way to qualify for an SHCA-presented-title based on meeting the requirements of performance in harness. These degrees—Sled Dog, Sled Dog Excellent, and Sled Dog Outstanding—as well as the Sled Dog classes offered at Specialties, allow the Siberian community to recognize the accomplishments of our dogs excelling on the trail.

More recently, there has been concern among the dog fancy, in general, to make sure judges are well educated about the breeds they judge. SHCA has taken this challenge seriously in producing several official educational programs. These programs are based on the Siberian Husky Standard, and include a slide presentation, discussion, the opportunity to apply the Standard to live dogs, correct proportion and movement, ringside mentoring, and a number of printed materials. These programs, although developed for judges, are equally of importance to breeders, exhibitors, and other fanciers. After all, it is the Standard to which breeders should breed, exhibitors wish to showcase, and judges use in evaluating their choices.

In the 1990s, one of the main concerns for purebred dog owners is the overpopulation of their breed, and the efforts to rescue no-longer-wanted dogs. SHCA started its Rescue Committee in response to this situation. Although run on a national level, SHCA Rescue helps local rescue groups by providing a framework, documentation, and process for their activities; funding; networking; and national contact. Additionally, SHCA Rescue helps in urgent situations by providing emergency funds in serious cases requiring immediate rescue and response. Thanks to this national framework partnering with the local network of caring, hundreds of no-longer-wanted Siberian Huskies have been saved.

Always looking for additional media to reach the Siberian community, SHCA got "wired" in 1996. The Internet address for the Siberian Husky Club of America, Inc., is http://www.shca.org. Since first establishing its web site, SHCA has received over 200,000 visitors, an average of more that 300 visits per day. This gives SHCA an additional opportunity to provide information about the Siberian to people in the United States and around the world.

As we approach the next millennium, the Siberian Husky is no longer solely the New England sled dog. This breed is found throughout the United States, and its popularity grows every day around the world. The Siberian Husky has been the most popular dog breed in Japan and Italy, and is high on the popularity lists in many other countries as well. Although SHCA's charter is to serve the Siberian community in the United States, the Club has been quick to respond to fellow fanciers in other countries. Some SHCA educational programs have been presented in a number of countries and many SHCA educational materials have been translated into other languages. And SHCA now includes a welcome committee for foreign visitors at its national Specialties.

Of course, the most obvious role of a Parent Club is to be the guardian of the Breed Standard. The initial Siberian Standard was written to describe a working sled dog. Over the years, SHCA has revised that Standard very few times. With each revision, however, the workability of the breed still is paramount, as it was to those who drafted the first Standard. Each revision attempted to clarify the picture the Standard paints of the Siberian. The ideal Siberian Husky described in that first Standard should be no stranger to the current version.

What is in store for the Siberian Husky and SHCA in the 2000s? Only time will tell. However, one thing is certain: As the breed develops needs, the Siberian Husky Club of America will continue trying to meet those needs.

RALPH LAUREN
PAINT

NEW ZEALAND COLLECTION

(Francois Helard)

CHAPTER 15

Siberians in the Media

BY PAT TETRAULT

Let's face it—advertisers LOVE to use dogs, because they attract the attention of prospective buyers to their products. In 1984, while working my second Siberian in Obedience, I really became aware of dogs in the media. So I asked around about how to get started and got some helpful advice, sending my dog's resumes off to the animal agencies in New York City. Months went by and I heard nothing. Then one day at an Obedience Trial where we were particularly successful (scoring 195 out of a possible 200), an agent approached me, stating, "There aren't many Siberians that can work off leash, you know"—that was it! Our career was launched.

That dog was Irlocon Eric's Little Erika, CDX, CGC, Can. CD. Now 16, Erika was seen on *The Late Show with David Letterman,* in countless commercials, and print advertisements. Although this sounds like a glamorous career, it really is a lot of hard work! A typical day for us entailed driving to a studio in Manhattan (the location varies—some jobs are done "on location" outside of New York). After struggling with traffic, finding a garage to park in (that accepts vans!), it is time to get busy with the actual work. When you arrive at the studio, most often you will sit for hours, waiting for "your turn." The ONLY time they are ready for you right away is when you are late!

As you prepare to bring your dog on the set, there are many things to think about and remember— are they working on white paper? Time to quickly clean your dog's feet and remove your shoes. Is the

185

"Flying high": Obedience stars become media stars: Pat Tetrault's Can. Ch. Khetaqua's One Hundred Proof, Am., Can. CD, TT, CgC (Stoli, left) and Am., Can. Ch. Stoli's Malinka Volchista, CGC (Linka, right). (Jerry Scheffler)

pedestal they want your dog to sit on secure? Your dog's safety is your responsibility at all times. How many photographs do you think are taken for a single ad? Often it is between eight and ten rolls of film! That's over 100 photographs! Can you as the "handler" sit back and relax during the shoot? Sorry, it's your job to keep the dog's attention focused, have it sit just so, keep the coat brushed, and keep an eye on the dog to see when it needs a break—studio lights are quite hot. It's hard work for both you and the dog!

Some of the jobs we've done have been fun AND funny. Our first major ad campaign was for Sargeant's™ flea collars. The ad was to depict a technician counting the "dead" fleas that had fallen off the dog (Erika). Well, the fleas were actually poppy seeds, and everything was going quite well until Erika sneezed and blew the fake fleas all away, ruining the makeup on the bald technician's

head in the process. Fortunately, we all had a good laugh over that one! I held my breath during one commercial—filming was done on the rooftop of a skyscraper. A few details were left out when the agency booked the dog. For example, I wasn't told that the dog had to be *carried* up a ladder for the final 12-foot climb, and that there was *no* safety rail around this building that was at least thirty stories high, and that the dog would be working off leash. Fortunately, the action called for the dog to lie down at the actress' feet and be fed shrimp linguine. Food is a wonderful motivator.

Working with Sigourney Weaver in a commercial for Japanese TV was also amusing—Erika was supposed to "talk" to Sigourney—the original plan was for her to howl and technicians would then dub in the voice. The instructions: have her howl for three seconds straight, stop for two seconds, and howl for an additional two seconds. Okay,

Erika—are you watching the clock! (We finally got the desired results for the producers after I suggested putting peanut butter on Erika's gums.)

Unfortunately, it's typical for the "writers" to have unrealistic expectations from our dogs. Linka (Am., Can. Ch. Stoli's Malinka Volchista, CD, CGC) was to provide the "seamless transition" from "The Tonight Show (with Jay Leno)" to "The Conan O'Brian Show." Her job? To take a pair of drumsticks from Leno's drummer, and deliver them to Max, Conan O'Brian's drummer. Sounds easy for a dog that enjoys retrieving, right? The writer asked if Linka would be able to "perform" on her own after a few run-throughs. The catch was that the studios are separated by two floors and a maze of corridors and doorways. Even I would get lost with only a few times to learn! Besides, I pointed out, how would the cameraman keep up with a running Siberian? With a few suggestions on both sides, the skit turned out to be so cute that Conan requested an ovation for the dog at the start of his live show!

"Stoli" (Can. Ch. Khetaqua's One Hundred Proof, Am.,Can CD, CGC, TT) was featured in a series of Ralph Lauren ads in the fall of 1997. Her first assignment was to be on a down/stay in the Ralph Lauren showroom as the new collection was unveiled to Mr. Lauren himself! When he entered the showroom and saw Stoli, he thought she was a stuffed dog

Stoli "on deck" during a Ralph Lauren shoot.

until she lifted her head and opened her big blue eyes for him. It was such a success that we were invited back for the "opening" of the showroom and hired to have her appear in an international ad campaign.

Candid shot at a Ralph Lauren showroom.

THE SMALL SCREEN BECKONS

Other people have had great success with their Siberians in the media. Stella Walker of KeeKaWa Siberians in Canada writes:

In October 1994, KeeKaWa's Kaery-Anne began her acting career with Lincoln as one of two Siberian Huskies playing the part of Diefenbaker on the television series *Due South*. The trainers had recognized the need for another Siberian Husky resembling Lincoln to join him in the role. In the series, Diefenbaker is a hearing-impaired, lip-reading, half-wolf sidekick to Constable Benton Fraser, a member of the Royal Canadian Mounted Police assigned to the Canadian Consulate in Chicago.

Kaery-Anne had been bred the day before the agreement was made for her to join the Dief Team. The trainers felt that this would be the opportune time to train her and prepare her for the role. Keeping in mind that she was pregnant, she was treated with tender loving care. Kaery-Anne went on maternity leave during Christmas and gave birth to KeeKaWa's MacKenzie King, known as MacKenzie and Ch KeeKaWa's Southern Treasure, known as Fraser. The puppies had their acting debut in the series during one episode where a love affair between Diefenbaker and a Siberian Husky named Maggie took place. Maggie, who played the role of the puppies' mother, was portrayed by another

On another job, two of my dogs appear in a greeting card (and poster) entitled "Top Dog." Ten dogs of all breeds are stacked, one on top of the other in a cheerleader-style pyramid. When folks ask how I got Stoli and Erika to do that, my standard reply is "Plexiglas"! In actuality, the dogs are stacked with the magic of computer enhancement.

"On Break"—Siberian style!

"Ah, the glamorous life": a candid study of Stoli taken during his Ralph Lauren modeling assignment.

KeeKaWa Siberian, Ch. Innisfree's Keeley Walker, CD. As the puppies grew, MacKenzie appeared on the TV series, joining Kaery-Anne and Lincoln as Diefenbaker. Totally, seven KeeKaWa-bred Siberians have appeared in *Due South*.

Kaery-Anne was popular with the dog trainers because they found her easy to work with. In one scene, Kaery-Anne, a chowhound by nature, walked up a set of stairs in the police station to the landing, past an actor who was eating a hamburger, and then proceeded up the second set of stairs. This, among other directives, she was able to master in one take. The first fan mail that came in for the show was for Diefenbaker. Dief had really captured the hearts of the audience. They loved the half-wolf. One admirer named "Puppy," who signed his letter with a big paw print wrote: "You are my big handsome hero." The show received phone calls, letters, and complaints on *Due South*'s Internet file if Diefenbaker received too little or no screen time at all.

In 1996, CBS wanted to cancel the series, but it was revived due to the overwhelming response of fans on the Internet. In 1997, *Due South* was finally canceled and Kaery-Anne returned home, while MacKenzie remained with one of the show's stunt men.

KeeKaWa's Kaery-Anne played "Diefenbaker" on the TV series Due South.

Our Siberians appear with regularity in the media. We never know what they'll be asked to do—one day it's howling, the next it might be cuddling in a model's lap. It's a business that is both interesting and frustrating, fun and funny, but most of all it's rewarding. How many people can say that they get paid to spend the day working with their dog?

(Frank and Marilyn Zanotti)

Titles for Which Siberian Huskies Are Eligible

OBEDIENCE TITLES: AKC

CD—Companion Dog

CDX—Companion Dog Excellent

UD—Utility Dog

UDX—Utility Dog Excellent

OTCH—Obedience Trial Champion

SLED DOG TITLES: SHCA

SD—Sled Dog

SDX—Sled Dog Excellent

SDO—Sled Dog Outstanding

FLYBALL TITLES

FD—Flyball Dog

FDX—Flyball Dog Excellent

FDCh—Flyball Dog Champion

FM—Flyball Master

FMX—Flyball Master Excellent

FMCh—Flyball Master Champion

ONYX—ONYX Award

FGDCh—Flyball Grand Champion

TRACKING TITLES

TD—Tracking Dog

TDX—Tracking Dog Excellent

VST—Variable Surface Tracking

AGILITY TITLES: AKC

NA—Novice Agility

OA—Open Agility

AX—Agility Excellent

MX—Master Agility Excellent

MACh—Master Agility Champion

NAJ—Novice Agility Jumpers

OAJ—Open Agility Jumpers

AXJ—Agility Excellent Jumpers

MXJ—Master Agility Excellent Jumpers

AGILITY TITLES: UKC

UAgI—Agility Level 1

U-AgII—Agility Level 2

U-ACH—Agility Champion

U-ACHX—Agility Champion Excellent

AGILITY TITLES: USDAA

AD—Agility Dog

VAD—Veteran Agility Dog

AAD—Advanced Agility Dog

VAAD—Veteran Advanced Agility Dog

MAD—Master Agility Dog

VMAD—Veteran Master Agility Dog

SM—Snooker Master

VS—Veteran Snooker

GM—Gambler Master

VG—Veteran Gambler

RM—Relay Master

JM—Jumpers Master

VJ—Veteran Jumpers

ADCH—Agility Dog Champion

VPD—Veteran Performance Dog

AGILITY TITLES: CANADA

ADC—Agility Dog of Canada

AADC—Advanced Agility Dog of Canada

MADC—Master Agility Dog of Canada

AGILITY TITLES: NADAC

(Each of these title has three divisions: the "standard" title; a veterans title for an older dog [with "V" after it]; and, a junior handler title for the kids [with a "JH" after it].)

NAC—Novice Agility

O-NAC—Outstanding Performance Novice Agility

S-NAC—Superior Performance Novice Agility

NGC—Novice Gamblers

O-NGC—Outstanding Performance Novice Gamblers

S-NGC—Superior Performance Novice Gamblers

NJC—Novice Jumpers

O-NJC—Outstanding Performance Novice Jumpers

OAC—Open Agility

O-OAC—Outstanding Performance Open Agility

S-OAC—Superior Performance Open Agility

OGC—Open Gamblers

O-OGC—Outstanding Performance Open Gamblers

S-OGC—Superior Performance Open Gamblers

OJC—Open Jumpers

O-OJC—Outstanding Performance Open Jumpers

S-OJC—Superior Performance Open Jumpers

EAC—Elite Agility

O-EAC—Outstanding Performance Elite Agility

S-EAC—Superior Performance Elite Agility

EGC—Elite Gamblers

O-EGC—Outstanding Performance Elite Gamblers

S-EGC—Superior Performance Elite Gamblers

EJC—Elite Jumpers

O-EJC—Outstanding Performance Elite Jumpers

S-EJC—Superior Performance Elite Jumpers

NATCH—North American Agility Trial Champion

O-NATCH—Outstanding Performance North American Agility Trial Champion

S-NATCH—Superior Performance North Agility Trial Champion

WORKING TITLES: SHCA

WPD—Working Pack Dog

WPDX—Working Pack Dog Excellent

National Specialty Winners and Owners

NATIONAL SPECIALTY WINNERS AND OWNERS

YEAR	DOG'S NAME	OWNER(S)
1989	Ch. Krykan's Alpha Centauri	Candis Criner and Patricia Marin
1990	Ch. Kontoki's Dennis The Menace	Wisniewski, Marcy, Oelshlager
1991	Ch. Tymberlyne's Echo Call Vegas	Michael J. Burnside
1992	Ch. Arcticlight's Robert Redfurred	R. & J. MacWade and Eric Van Loo
1993	Ch. Kolya of the Midnight Sun	Harry Keefe and Janis Church
1994	Ch. Kontoki's E-I-E-I-O	Wisniewski, Moye, DePalma, Oelschlager
1995	Ch. Wildestar's Fire N' Ice	Brenda and Albert Valletta
1996	Ch. Tazoric's Stars And Stripes	William Campbell
1997	Ch. Highlander's Tool Time	Holly Potter and Anne Taber
1998	Ch. Wildestar's Cat Ballou	Brenda and Albert Valletta

(JoLynn Stresing)

A P P E N D I X   C

Additional Resources— Books and Organizations

Books, General Information

Craige, Patricia. *Born to Win: Breed to Succeed.* Wilsonville, Ore.: Doral Publishing, Inc., 1997.

Elliott, Rachel Page. *The New Dogsteps.* New York: Howell Book House, 1983.

International SHC, Inc. *The Siberian Husky.* Spake Printing, 1994.

Kanzler, Kathleen. *A New Owner's Guide to Siberian Huskies.* Neptune City, N.J.: TFH Publications, 1996.

Meador, Debbie. *Top Producers: Siberian Huskies, The Family Album.* Centerville, VA: Denlinger's Publishers, 1985.

Rickcr, Elizabeth M. *Seppala—Alaskan Dog Driver.* New York: Little, Brown, 1931 reprint.

Tanner, John Douglas, Jr. *Alaskan Trails—Siberian Dogs.* Whcat Ridge, CO: Hoflin Publ., Ltd., 1998.

BOOKS, BREEDING AND HEALTH

Battaglia, Carmen. *Breeding Better Dogs.* Roswell, GA: Battaglia Enterprises, 1960.

Carlson, Delbert, and James M. Giffin. *The Dog Owner's Home Veterinary Handbook.* New York: Howell Book House, 1992.

Evans, J. M., and Kay White. *The Book of the Bitch.* New York: Howell Book House, 1997.

Finder-Harris, Beth J. *Breeding a Litter.* New York: Howell Book House, 1993.

Rice, Dan. *The Complete Book of Dog Breeding.* Hauppauge, N.Y.: Barron's Educational Series, 1996.

Walkowicz, Chris. *Successful Dog Breeding.* New York: Howell Book House, 1994.

BOOKS, SLEDDING

Cary, Bob, and Gail de Marcken. *Born to Pull.* Pfeifer-Hamilton, 1998.

Collins, Miki, and Julie Collins. *Riding the Wild Side of Denali, Alaska Adventure With Horses and Huskies.* Epicenter Press, 1998.

Cook, Ann Mariah. *Running North, A Yukon Adventure.* Algonquin, 1998.

Coppinger, Lorna, with the International Sled Dog Racing Association. *The World of Sled Dogs.* New York: Howell Book House, 1972.

Fishback, Lee. *Training Lead Dogs.* Nunica, Mich.: Tun-Ora, 1978.

Flanders, Noel K. *The Joy of Running Sled Dogs.* Loveland, CO: Alpine Publications, 1989.

Freedman, Lewis, and illustrated by Jon Van Zyle. *Iditarod Classics.* Epicenter Press, 1992.

The International Siberian Husky Club. *The Siberian Husky.* Elkhorn, WI: Spake Printing Services, Inc., 1994.

Jonrowe, DeeDee, and Lewis Freedman. *Iditarod Dreams.* Epicenter Press, 1995.

Paulsen, Gary. *Winterdance.* Harcourt, 1995.

———. *Woodsong.* Puffin, 1991.

Ramsey, James. *Winter Watch.* Graphics Art Center, 1989.

Scott, Alastair. *Tracks Across Alaska: A Dog Sled Journey.* Atlantic Monthly Press, 1991.

Shields, Mary. *Sled Dog Trails.* Pyrola, 1984.

Welch, Jim. *The Speed Mushing Manual.* Sirius, 1989.

BOOKS, CHILDREN'S

Bacon, Ethel. *To See the Moon.* Bridgewater, 1996.

Blake, Robert J. *Akiak: A Tale from the Iditarod.* Philomel Books, 1997.

Gil, Shelley. *Kiana's Iditarod.* Paws IV, 1992.

Morey, Walt. *Kavik, the Wolf Dog.* Dutton, 1997.

Paulsen, Gary. *Dogteam.* Delacorte Press, 1993.

———. *Puppies, Dogs, and Blue Northers, Reflections on Being Raised by a Pack of Sled Dogs.* Harcourt, Brace, Jovanovich, 1996.

Riddles, Libby, and Shelley Gill. *Danger, the Dog Yard Cat.* Paws IV, 1995.

Riddles, Libby. *Storm Run.* Paws IV, 1996.

Shields, Mary. *The Alaskan Happy Dog Trilogy: Can Dogs Talk?; Loving a Happy Dog; Secret Messages.* Pyrola, 1991.

BOOKS, TRAINING

Benjamin, Carol Lea. *Mother Knows Best.* New York: Howell Book House, 1985.

The Monks of New Skete. *The Art of Raising a Puppy.* Little, Brown, 1991.

Pryor, Karen. *Don't Shoot the Dog: The New Art of Teaching and Training.* Bantam, 1985.

Rutherford, Clarise, and David H. Neil. *How To Raise A Puppy You Can Live With.* Loveland, CO: Alpine Publications, 1992.

Vollmer, Peter J. *SuperPuppy.* Escondido, Cal.: SuperPuppy Press, 1992.

SIBERIAN HUSKY CLUB OF AMERICA EDUCATIONAL MATERIALS

"A Partnership for Life: Learning to Understand Your Siberian Husky"

"The Siberian Husky Club of America Information Booklet"

"Your Siberian Husky: Its Hips and Eyes"

Hurley, Fay Clark. "Siberian Huskies," *Pure-Bred Dogs—American Kennel Gazette,* 1931.

New Standards Approved. *Pure-Bred Dogs—American Kennel Gazette,* April 1, 1932.

Siberian Husky Club of America, Inc. Constitution and By-Laws, May 4, 1995.

Siberian Husky Club of America, Inc. Membership Application.

Siberian Husky Club of America, Inc. Code of Ethics.

NOTE: These and other SHCA materials are available from the Corresponding Secretary, Fain Zimmerman, 210 Madera Drive, Victoria, TX 77905-0611.

Further information is updated regularly on the SHCA web site: *http://www.shca.org.*

VIDEOS

The best video sources are in dog product catalogs. These titles are from Black Ice, New Germany, Minnesota.

Alaska's Great Race: The Susan Butcher Story.

Balto.

Dogsledding In Wisconsin, Trailside Videos.

Dunbar, Dr. Ian, *Sirius Puppy Training.*

Elliott, Rachel Page, *Dogsteps: A Study of Canine Structure and Movement.*

Rutherford, Clarise, and David H. Neil, *How To Raise A Puppy You Can Live With.*

Shield, Mary, *Season of the Sled Dog.*

Warren, Susan, *Introduction to Skijoring.*

Race For Life, Gospel Films.

Racing the Wind, KYUK Productions.

Winter Patrol: Denali by Dog Sled.

DOG SLEDDING OUTFITTERS

Black Ice Dog Sledding Equipment
3620 Yancy Avenue
New Germany, MN 55367
(320) 485-4825

Cold Spot Feeds/The Real Alaska Mushing
   Company (RAMCO)
471 Fleshman Street
Fairbanks, AK 99712
(907) 457-8555

Raels Harness Shop
401 West International Airport Road
Anchorage, AK 99518
(907) 563-3411

Resha Dog Sledding Equipment
HC 1, Box 101
Lewis Run, PA 16738
(814) 362-3048

Risdon Rogs
P.O. Box 127
Laingsburg, MI 48848
(517) 651-6960

Taiga Mushing Supplies
388 Reynolds Lane
Fairbanks, AK 99712
(907) 488-7641

Mushing
P.O. Box 149
Ester, AK 99725

Mush with P.R.I.O.E.—Sled Dog Care Guidelines
P.O. Box 84915
Fairbanks, AK 99708

INTERNET SITES

http://amazon.com

American Kennel Club
   http://www.akc.org

http://www.barnesandnoble.com

Rae's Harness Shop
   http://www.alaskan.com/raes/raes.html
   (for sledding equipment)

Siberian Husky Club of America
   http://www.shca.org

Sled Dog Central
   http://www.sleddogcentral.com
   (for advertising and information)

NOTE: The Internet is the best source for current information regarding any book, i.e., availability, price, reviews, how to acquire out-of-print materials, etc. It is updated regularly and direct orders for home delivery are easily placed.

EPILOGUE

The Color of the Siberian

At the risk of sounding trite, writing a "color" book on the Siberian Husky was truly a labor of love, but with a special dimension. Because color plays so vital a role in the beauty and allure of the breed—the drama of the high contrast shades, the subtlety of the lighter, more delicately nuanced tones—it's part of what makes each individual seem so wonderfully unique. Along with markings, body language, temperament, and personality, color helps define the Siberian Husky. In fact, few Siberians seem to have much doubt about their individuality, their "personhood." I've known hounds that clearly worried about whether they were good hounds, retrievers clearly fretful about whether they were good enough retrievers. But most Siberians seem to know from the start that they're Siberians, and that's good enough for them. And it had better be good enough for you, because they're not about to pretend to be Lassie or Fido. I remember someone in a book advising that one should lend oneself to others but give oneself to oneself, and that strikes me now as very Siberian. Our Siberians love us, certainly, but certainly not exclusively or obsessively. Sometimes they even appear to forget we exist. And I love that about them, their cocky independence and apparent *savoir faire*. The world seems always to be pretty much their oyster, except maybe when you're having dinner and they're not.

But I also love the intensity with which they do lend themselves to us—if we can manage to get their attention—whether in harness (which they take to instinctively and obsessively), obedience, the

203

show ring, the agility ring, or the back-packing or skijoring trail. When working well in any of these interspecies activities, the Siberian lends us his ancient magic, his ancient gifts of focus and endurance, his pure pleasure in the task, and foolish-pleasure clowning at the completion of a task (at least we hope he waits 'til the completion of the task). And when that happens we enter his story, the story of one of the world's most beautiful and most ancient working dogs whose original people fostered and depended on him for their very survival.

Like Indian ponies at dawn: variety of coat color and markings makes every Siberian an original. (JoLynn Stresing)

Sadly, of course, the tremendous physical beauty of the Siberian Husky lures many people to him who will never be comfortable with his temperament, who find there's a certain "chaos factor" somewhat at odds with Persian carpets and fine collectibles. Designerly as they may appear, in other words, Siberians seldom suit a "designer" lifestyle, or even a family with a very busy, tightly scheduled life. SIBERIANS ARE A LOT OF TROUBLE; that's the long and short of it. This means they need a lot of attention.

Those of us hooked on them, on the other hand, treasure that "chaos factor" (at least, most of the time). It feels something like "irrepressible life-force" or some such Luke Skywalker term. It usually makes us laugh because it makes us rethink things for a moment. It turns the universe on its head, so to speak, because it reminds us that ours is not the only reality. These wonderful dogs, too, have a reality, probably much older than ours, certainly much more aligned with the immediate environment. And when seen from that vantage point, most of the unexpected antics of Siberians make sense. They just see and experience a little differently, often in ways clearly "wolfish." Because Siberians are, as Connie Miller the anthropologist once pointed out, "infantilized wolves"—they maintain many of the physical and behavioral characteristics of wolf cubs into adulthood (their head planes, for instance, and much of their temperament). But even an infantilized wolf is a pretty smart animal, smart enough to have been self-sufficient during the warmer months in their native Siberia, smart enough to have often been self-reliant, even heroic, in harness before generations of snow-blind drivers, and smart enough to sometimes outsmart us, their owners. And that's humbling, and laughable, and probably very healthy—even therapeutic. It makes us a little more like their partners than their masters, even if we are good "pack leaders."

I was recently asked by the *AKC Gazette* to write about the "essence" of the Siberian Husky. It came to me like this:

ESSENCE OF SIBERIAN

1 part wolf, 1 part vagabond, 1 part court jester, 1 part fairytale fox, 1 part mystic snow-Buddha, 1 part lounge lizard (sometimes in tux or tails), 1 part anarchist, 1 part Puss N' Boots, 1 part Crown Prince, 1 part Artful Dodger, 1 part sheer guts and determination:
Shaken or stirred; sugar, salt or paprika to taste.

Let's keep him this way—a free spirit, a beautiful NATURAL breed, an able athlete, an able friend.

Index